Praises for
Jesus: He Who is, Who was, and Who is to Come.

It is a concise book that uses bible history to provide the plan of salvation by showing God's divinity, our need for God, the coming of the end days, and what happens to those in the Church who compromise on what the Word of God says.
—**Freda Kramer**

***

Very informative as to Christian teachings and Christian beliefs. Very informative as to living a Christian life.
—**Tom Kearney**

***

I would highly recommend this book. In a world of iniquity, Christians need to make a stand, and that is what this book does.

For we wrestle not against flesh and blood, but against principalities, against powers, against the rulers of the darkness of this world, against spiritual wickedness in high places (Ephesians 6:12).
—**Keenan Burns**

***

The introduction has captured my attention and I believe the book is evoking us as Christians to take a deeper look...encouraging us to take a stand for God. The way it connects biblical history with the current events of today is wonderful and encouraging. This book connects the truth and facts from our history to our current situation and encourages fellow Christians to stand up for our Lord and Savior - our God is a loving and forgiving God, but He also holds us accountable as our Father and His children whom He sacrificed and lovingly gave His life for that we might know/have eternal life.

In Christian Love,
—**Ms. Vivian Starling**

***

This is a good read, would help the saved and unsaved. Many are falling away for lack of Godly wisdom, turning a blind eye to all the evil before us each day. We need to have hope in Jesus Christ.
—**Charles Spradley**

***

It was my privilege to read this book, which was clearly inspired by the Holy Spirit and evident in the words that were written on each page. You can feel his desire to tell the gospel story; explaining that we were born into sinful nature and saved by the grace of God through Jesus's sacrificial offering of himself to become sin, he who had no sin, to save and redeem mankind, who was created in God's image.

The book did a great job of comparing events of old to modern-day times, showing how God never changes, and HE is the only constant in this world. We are truly living in a time that reflects the Babylonian era, which God wiped out once already because of the arrogant sin of humans and idol worship.

The book is packed full of scripture and truths, backed up by the authenticity of the Bible, God's Holy and Divine Word.

The research and the analogies that are in each chapter lay out God's character and the gospel of Jesus Christ. I love the story about grandpa and his life-long experiences here on earth. He told many stories about traditions of his day and all the advances in technology over the past 100 years, which seems unreal when you consider it's divided by only one generation. This shows how important eyewitnesses are to our future because if these stories (real-life events) are not documented and retold, the generations to come will never know the whole picture; like the example of the cousin, who had never heard of cars without electric windows or the fact that Bibles were used as legal documents to prove births before there were birth certificates.

The book emphasized the true nature of sin, in that sin is rooted in pride and envy. "For instance, the bible teaches man looks at the outward appearance, but God looks at the heart." He lays out how Satan was at one time a high-standing angel of God but pride led him astray, wanting others to worship him over God. Therefore, he became a fallen angel and was cast out of God's presence, with those that he recruited to follow him. Then Satan deceived Adam and Eve in the garden of Eden, which was the fall of man and sin entered into the world. God gave Adam and Eve free will and everything they could possibly need... but they wanted the one thing God warned them not to touch.

God wants a relationship, not a dictatorship... All creatures were created to worship him, even the birds wake up singing and praising their creator.

Beautifully written... "Isn't it ironic people would see the glory and majesty and beauty of creation with the eyes that God gave them as a wonderful window to view the splendor of a sunrise against a marvelous canvas sky and then lose sight of the light of the Almighty. The light of thankfulness for the rain and food God provides, and the light of the fact the very breath and health and strength of a person depend upon God's sustaining power, by Him we live and move and have our being."

Indeed, a reminder of God's sovereignty and how quickly we can take him for granted and think that we know what's best for our lives, instead of the creator himself.

"The horrific scars of the holocaust should serve as a warning against evil empires who feel their military strength or technological advancement make them untouchably empowered to destroy innocent lives for their own twisted agendas. These people committing these terrible unthinkable atrocities on innocent people were highly intelligent and being led by perpetrators willing to deceive their own people by covering what they were doing or misleading them through propaganda to passively stand by or even more troubling actively engage in the killing of innocent people because of twisted ideologies and principles like only the strong survive evolutionary lies." Unfortunately, some of what happened in Germany has already happened in the United States and if it continues, the scars will be permanent in America, which is supposed to be the land of the free and the home of the brave.

My prayer is to see this book published so that it will encourage others to seek and stand on the truth before it is too late. May God bless this book for the courage and dedication to share the love of Christ and live out the Great Commission!

Matthew 28:18-20 KJV
- **18** And Jesus came and spake unto them, saying, All power is given unto me in heaven and in earth.
- **19** Go ye therefore, and teach all nations, baptizing them in the name of the Father, and of the Son, and of the Holy Ghost:
- **20** Teaching them to observe all things whatsoever I have commanded you: and, lo, I am with you always, even unto the end of the world. Amen.

—Doris Redish

JESUS

HE WHO IS, WHO WAS, AND WHO IS TO COME

JOHN CREEL

Published by KHARIS PUBLISHING, imprint of KHARIS MEDIA LLC.

Copyright © 2022 John Creel

ISBN-13: 978-1-63746-111-2

ISBN-10: 1-63746-111-9

Library of Congress Control Number: 2022931802

All rights reserved. This book or parts thereof may not be reproduced in any form, stored in a retrieval system, or transmitted in any form by any means - electronic, mechanical, photocopy, recording, or otherwise - without prior written permission of the publisher, except as provided by United States of America copyright law.

All Scripture quotations, unless otherwise indicated, are taken from the KING JAMES VERSION (KJV): KING JAMES VERSION, public domain.

All KHARIS PUBLISHING products are available at special quantity discounts for bulk purchase for sales promotions, premiums, fund-raising, and educational needs. For details, contact:

Kharis Media LLC
Tel: 1-479-599-8657
support@kharispublishing.com
www.kharispublishing.com

TBALE OF CONTENTS

He Who Is ix
    Authenticity of the Scriptures/Chronologically Correct/
    Archaeological Evidence Aligning with Scripture 1
    Geological Proof of His Power 6
    Historical Significance 9
    The Mayflower Compact 13

He Who Was 15
    Prophetic Reliability 16
    Gods' Stamp of Approval 21
    Knowledge of the Truth 24
    Timeline of Righteousness and Judgment 27

He who is to Come 57
    Who to Trust 58
    When the Angels Reap 79
    Chosen 104

References 115
About Kharis Publishing: 116

HE WHO IS

Authenticity of the Scriptures/Chronologically Correct/ Archaeological Evidence Aligning with Scripture

Revelation chapter one verse eight states: I am Alpha and Omega, the beginning and the ending, saith the **Lord, which is, and which was, and which is to come, the Almighty**. Proof & authenticity of the scriptures have been verified throughout the ages as accurate and true. The very writing of Jewish history in the holy texts reveals an entire office and possibly multiple offices which were dedicated to the procurement and preservation of their sacred history as the chosen people by the Most High God, the God of Abraham, Isaac, and Jacob, as well as the God and Father of our Lord Jesus Christ.

The Bible.org (2020) explains the incredible chronological balance of the scriptural record in an overview as follows; the first five books of the Bible are sometimes called the Pentateuch which means "five books." They are also known as the books of the law because they contain the laws and instruction given by the Lord through Moses to the people of Israel. These books were written by Moses, except for the last portion of Deuteronomy because it tells about the death of Moses. These five books lay the foundation for the coming of Christ in that here God chooses and brings into being the nation of Israel. As God's chosen people, Israel became the custodians of the Old Testament, the recipients of the covenants of promise, and the channel of Messiah (Rom. 3:2; 9:1-5).

Additionally, scribes and recorders are mentioned in the Old Testament, specifically in Second Samuel chapter eight versus fifteen through seventeen which states "And David reigned over all Israel, and David executed judgment and justice unto all his people. And Joab the son of Zeruiah was over the host; and Jehoshaphat the son of Ahilud was recorder; And Zadok the son of Ahitub, and Ahimelech the son of Abiathar, were the priests; and Seraiah was the scribe; (KJV Online, 2020)."

Therefore, as the Holy Bible is researched in its entirety, it is quickly and easily observed that the Old Testament was a history lesson of God's creation. God's creation of the heavens and the earth, as well as Adam and Eve, along with His hand of grace toward Noah, destruction by the flood because people's imaginations were only evil continually, God's choosing of Abraham as His friend, and the genealogy from Adam to Abraham which continued with a promise to Abraham and his seed.

His seed like many occasions throughout chosen generations and times, involved God working a miracle to reveal His glory (so no flesh could glory in His presence). Hebrews relates a similar part in 1:1 "God, who at sundry times and in divers manners spake in time past unto the fathers by the prophets," God chose Abraham and Sarah to bring forth a son in old age to bring to pass the promise they had so long awaited by faith. The promise and fulfillment of the promise was Isaac to Abraham and ultimately through their genealogical line the promise of Jesus Christ to be a savior to the children of Israel and miraculously to the entire world, Jews and Gentiles alike. For God so loved the world that He have his only begotten Son that whosoever believeth in Him should not perish but have everlasting life.

The Dead Sea Scrolls were one the most significant archaeological finds for the proof and validity of the ancient scriptures in modern history. The scrolls were found in the caves of Qumran near the Dead Sea. The Dead Sea Scrolls.org (2020) details the monumental discovery as follows. "East of the city of Jerusalem, the mountainous landscape plummets dramatically 1200 meters to the lowest point on earth, the Dead Sea. Some of the most dramatic biblical stories are set in the rocky caves of this region, between the Judean hills and the Dead Sea. Here, in the intense heat of the barren Judean Desert, we can visualize David fleeing from King Saul seeking refuge in the desert's mountain caves and Jesus rejecting the temptations of the devil. For thousands of years, the Judean Desert held secrets buried in its sands, only to be revealed by a young Bedouin shepherd in 1947. The discovery of these ancient treasures initiated a modern-day adventure into the past, revolutionizing our understanding of history...."

The scrolls range from the third century B.C. to A.D. seventy. The materials used for the scrolls were made up of mostly parchment, although some were papyrus and one engraved in copper. The scrolls verify the biblical texts by providing both partial and complete copies of every book in the Hebrew Bible (except the book of Esther). "They already held a special status in the Second Temple period and were considered to be vessels of divine communication (DSS, 2020)." So, historical and theological evidence of scriptural accuracy are vast and well circulated.

Now, the reliability of God's manuscript to man is reinforced through the overarching history, theme, and prophecy alignment throughout the old and New Testament. Amazingly, the many prophets who spake as they were moved by the holy ghost, as described in scripture as in second Peter as 2 Peter 1:21 "For the prophecy came not in old time by the will of man: but holy men of God spake as they were moved by the Holy Ghost (KJV Online, 2020)." Psalms 94: "He that planted the ear, shall he not hear? He that formed the eye, shall he not see?" A little deeper into the knowledge and greatness of the Almighty reveals His will in the salvation plan. The plan explains God's will in people who repent for the kingdom of God is at hand. This will in John 1:13 "Which were born, not of blood, nor of the will of the flesh, nor of the will of man, but of God." The bible teaches the fear of the Lord is the beginning of knowledge (Proverbs 9:10: The fear of the LORD is the beginning of wisdom: and the knowledge of the holy is understanding. Proverbs 1:7: The fear of the LORD is the beginning of knowledge: but fools despise wisdom and instruction.) The bible also teaches His ways are higher than our ways. God is a Spirit and they that worship Him must worship Him In Spirit and in truth, and that Jesus is the way the truth and the life. Jesus is the only name under heaven by which we must be saved.

A trial scene in the movie God's not Dead involved the research of a true cold case detective who went on a journey to discover the truth of the gospel using the same techniques used for examining testimony in cold cases. He concluded that if eyewitness testimony are too similar, they likely were coerced and scripted together and likely untrue. Next, if the testimony is too scattered they are likely fabricating the event. However, if the eyewitness testimony involves a different perspective of the same overarching theme with varying amounts of details provided about the scene or event, it is likely true testimony. His work involved around thirty years of experience using the investigative techniques. He found the testimony of the Gospels of Jesus Christ to be amazingly accurate by the fact that each explained what they saw of the same events with varied focus and perspectives which is exactly what happens when multiple people witness the same events.

Dead Sea Scrolls (Image below: dss.collections.imj.org.il)

Caves of Qumran (Image below: deadseascrolls.org.il)

Geological Proof of His Power

Others examine the major geological events which are recorded in the scriptures like the flood and the destruction of Sodom and Gomorrah. Answers in Genesis (2020) explain how research has revealed fossils of sea creatures in rock layers that cover all the continents. For example, most of the rock layers in the walls of the Grand Canyon (more than a mile above sea level) contain marine fossils. Fossilized shellfish are even found in the Himalayas. Of course, Genesis and John both explain creation and that all things were made by Him (Jesus) and for Him.

The bible is also very clear by Him we live and move and have our being, and to let everything that hath breath praise the Lord. He created the greater light to rule the day and the lesser light to rule the night in a single day during creation. His Word declares the heavens' His throne and the earth is His footstool. It also declares His greatness is unsearchable and His understanding infinite. Also, the Lord sits upon the circles of the earth even though many in history once thought it was flat. The truth was declared much earlier in the holy scripture, and even though He has to humble Himself to behold the things of earth, He has respect unto the lowly.

His truth also declares and teaches that it's in the heart of a king to search out a matter and that we should prove all things. So, yes the bible teaches the just shall live by faith. Scripture defines faith as follows: faith is the substance of things hoped for, the evidence of things not seen. This is very important to realize that evidence is a key component to the faith formula because the bible teaches we overcome by faith. Salvation in Jesus Christ also involves believing in our hearts unto righteousness and confessing with our mouths unto salvation. So, once we believe, it brings forth righteous actions. For example, John the Baptist taught the people to bring forth fruits worthy of repentance. Therefore, when a person repents of their sins and the blood of Jesus cleanses them from all unrighteousness, an incredible transformation takes place in the inward man.

Sometimes, depending upon the emotions or demeanor of the individual, a person may feel overwhelmingly happy or soberly calm and peaceful. The wonderful transformation involves God through His son Jesus redeeming men and women unto Himself. The Bible expounds on a key term called regeneration during this process. The first scripture helps to explain how powerful and eternally lasting the regeneration is. Matthew 19:28; And Jesus said unto them, Verily I say unto you, that ye which have followed me, in the regeneration when the Son of man shall sit in the throne of his glory, ye also shall sit upon twelve thrones, judging the twelve tribes of Israel. So, this scripture alludes to the world to come. Thus, aligning with the truth that the things which are seen are made by the things which are not seen. Our God is a consuming fire.

In fact, Israel's history reveals such a time after the exodus from Egypt while in the wilderness that God desired to help the people fear Him all their days by revealing Himself unto them. His plan involved descending upon the mountain in their sight. Now no man has seen God's face and lived but He was going to show them His mighty power and presence. However, once He gave Moses express instructions, He descended toward the mountain and the shaking, loud noise, and the mountain smoking caused the people to turn and hide while telling Moses you go up to the Lord.

The second time regeneration is visited in the New Testament, it was not the world to come by where the scripture teaches the kingdom of God comes without observation when asked about the revelation of the kingdom of God. So, it's clear Jesus was saying the kingdom of God is within you like a small seed planted in the heart and growing into a mighty tree.

Titus 3:5: Not by works of righteousness which we have done, but according to his mercy he saved us, by the washing of regeneration, and renewing of the Holy Ghost;

Amazing how God can completely change a person's life from within by regeneration and renewing of the Holy Ghost and all by the gift of righteousness, just by asking Jesus the son of God. In one instance, Jesus revealed His power while He was in the Flesh by asking a group that had gathered if He had power on earth to forgive sins. He proclaimed which is easier to say rise up and walk, or to say thy sins are forgiven thee that thou mayest know the Son of Man has power to forgive sin, and the man was made whole.

Sodom and Gomorrah was another recent study of a world event in scripture that has been studied which CBN (2018) released a study by researchers that went like this 'Temps as Hot as the Surface of the Sun:' Did Scientists Find Evidence of the Destruction of Biblical Sodom. Researchers found the place to be synonymous with the geographic region and the evidence of catastrophic proportion. The bible also warns about oppositions of science to the truth in

1 Timothy 6:20; O Timothy, keep that which is committed to thy trust, avoiding profane and vain babblings, and oppositions of science falsely so called:

So, how did people try and construe such a marvelous work of creation into because we can study what was already here, we can explain it with monkey motion. A leading anthropologist said we come from a fish's gill in an article and responded his reasoning for lack of a better answer. So, some people studying history and the earth's phenomenon's realized they cannot make a simple tree like God made in creation, but they can plant one. In other words, His eternal power and Godhead are clearly seen through His Creation, the things that He made so they are without excuse the bible teaches.

The heavens declare His handiwork, O Lord our Lord how excellent is thy name in all the earth. When I consider thy heavens and the work of Thy fingers, the moon and the stars which thou hast ordained what is man that thou art mindful of him and the son of man that Thou visitest him. The mystery is then revealed which has been hid from ages and generations which was brought to pass through Christmas, the birth of Jesus Christ, and his life, death, and resurrection, Christ in us the hope of glory.

Historical Significance

So how did we get to where we are now where some try and falsely match so called science against so called religion? The answer to how we got where we are today lies in history buried under pages and decades. Empires and events have played out over centuries to build upon times and lessons of generations past. The Roman Empire for instance which some may feel is the extension of the feet of iron and clay in the Daniel prophecy of Empires in his interpretation in Babylon. A kingdom vision of a He-goat was noted as the kingdom of Grecia, out of which would come the leader in the last days who is known as the beast. While some may discard America as part of that scenario, a closer look may add light. For instance, where iron doesn't mix with clay in the vision like a mixture of people or melting pot as put in American history, and America is an extension of Europe also called the old world which Greece and Alexander the great dominated and his kingdom split into four parts towards the four winds, or north, south, east, and west.

The European history of the middle ages is like a Q-beam exposing the dilemmas of that age which led to some of the current distresses. Two major events took place in the middle ages which affected nations, ideologies, and principles of future generations. Of course, Jesus has impacted the world more than any other person. The bible is the most sold and read book ever written. Our calendar and dating system revolve around his life interestingly enough like the Old Testament to New Testament. Before Christ (B.C.) was like the Old Testament where prophets proclaimed the Savior would appear and specific details of how He would appear as Isaiah detailed His sufferings and in the book of Psalms that the holy one would not see corruption because he would raise from the dead. The phrase Anno Domini (A.D.) denotes in the year of our Lord, so timely to the New

Testament which reveals the life, miracles, and good works of the savior to the world and fulfilled prophesies like the one illustrated in

Matthew 8:17; that it might be fulfilled which was spoken by Esaias the prophet, saying, Himself took our infirmities, and bare our sicknesses.

The two major events in the middle ages were the Reformation and the Enlightenment which both unfolded in Europe. The Roman Empire was a powerful kingdom which controlled much of the world from Europe to western Asia and North Africa and had dominion during the time of Jesus Christ. Of course, after Jesus' ascension the disciples of Jesus and Christianity grew mightily even under great persecution of the early church. Paul, who had once persecuted Christians but was converted after a vision on his way to Damascus, took the gospel all the way to Rome and before the Emperor Nero.

The gospel spread quickly throughout the Mediterranean into Europe. Incredibly, the once much persecuted Christianity became the faith of the entire Roman Empire in the three hundreds A.D. under the first Christian Emperor Constantine. The Roman Empire split into the Byzantine Empire in the east with its capital in Constantinople. The early three hundreds A.D. shifted power to the east while invaders further weakened the west with a power shift going to Germanic tribes in the four hundreds A.D. However, power was not the only shift as the Byzantine Empire took on a shift of views to Eastern Orthodox Christianity. Eastern Orthodox Christianity went from a papal or pope as leader to a patriarch and spread Christianity into Russia and Byzantium remained a dominant world power until the fourteen hundreds A.D.

Meanwhile, Charlemagne in the early eight hundreds on the western empire front, was a Frankish or German king who was crowned emperor of Rome by Pope Leo III on Christmas day. Charlemagne's military ambitions to convert the entire empire to Christianity reunited most of the old Western Roman Empire. These events set the stage for the middle ages in Europe. The Roman Catholic Church was the dominant political power which ran the government and empire during the Middle Ages and usually kings were subservient to the popes because if the pope refused communion to a king or excommunicated them the people would stand with the Church. Therefore, kings declared divine right as leaders to combat the power of the papacy. One king attempted a power grab from a pope in order to elect leaders in the Church and found himself kneeling and begging for repentance before the pope and the people so he could receive communion. This was due to the fact the Catholic tradition of the time required communion to be received in order for entry into heaven.

This brings us into the discussion of Church doctrine and biblical truth. The Catholic Church of the middle ages had many traditions not rooted in scripture. For Example, the selling of relics (bones of dead saints) for forgiveness of sins was common and proved to be a corrupting factor and deviation from foundational biblical Christianity. How did they veer so far off course so fast? The priests were educated in Latin and could read the scriptural texts and then dictate that to the people. This was at a time when most common people couldn't read Latin and had no available translation at the time which made them vulnerable to private interpretation which the bible warns against, along with traditions of men. Jesus warned the temple leaders of his day about how they had made void the Word of God by their traditions.

The Roman Catholic Church of the middle ages had officially corrupted. The problem was they controlled the government and the armies which were led by the popes themselves into battle. So, a German monk decided to write about the corruption and the true way to inherit eternal life. He pointed out the scripture of salvation by grace through faith not of works. Of course, he faced intense backlash and fled for his life into the countryside and into hiding. Amazingly, an incredible invention of that day brought about the printing press which proved to be the weapon for spreading the message throughout many regions. The concluding and long term result after the thirty years war and wars between Catholics and Protestants would result in a shift to a new continent.

Now the gospel of course is not isolated to one region or peoples on the Earth, even though Israel was and is and always will be elect for the Father's sake as God's chosen people and place on Earth to dwell in Zion. Jesus Christ the Son of the Living God was revealed in the last days to take away sin. This brings great hope for many important reasons. One important reason is that when sin is taken away Jesus (the way, the truth, and the life) makes a way or bridges the gap back to fellowship with our heavenly Father.

The bible teaches, so a man so is a nation. Therefore, a man or woman (mankind) have the opportunity to believe in the testimony that God gave of His Son that Jesus was the Son of God, and by faith be reconciled to right relations with their Heavenly Father. One of the biggest evidences of this redemption is within a person because the bible teaches that His Spirit bears witness with our spirit that we are the sons of God. Jesus warned precisely of the harsh reality of unpardonable judgment upon the soul of man who blasphemes the Holy Ghost during an exchange in which some falsely claimed He had an evil spirit. The Holy Spirit has a magnificent way of striving with the hearts and minds of men and women, boys and girls to show them just how much he loves and cares for them. He would that none should perish but all should come to the knowledge of the truth. Hell was made for the devil and his angels not for man, so man has to choose to reject the mighty love of Jesus Christ by His sacrifice and death on a cruel cross to redeem man by His blood.

Honestly, such a sacrifice for someone would be very difficult to even think about, much less follow through with, for those who had ridiculed, spit, slapped, blasphemed, mocked, and hurt Him. A song about the love of God declares how fathomless is this love, be reconciled to God. Interestingly, God could have easily dominated the will of mankind by forcing them to serve him for their own good and procurement. However, one of the most astounding verses in all of the Holy Scriptures states whosoever will let him come. "Let him," is a liberating choice of true freedom to come to God.

The God of all creation, the God of whom the heaven is His throne and the Earth is His footstool. The God who inhabits eternity and has to humble Himself to behold the things of the Earth and yet He delights in a poor and contrite spirit. The God in whose image we were and are made. The God who knows the thoughts He has toward us, thoughts of peace and not of evil, to give us an expected end. The God whose thoughts toward you are more than the sands of the seas, and who first loved you, He chose you.

The Old Testament treasure chest reveals a time when God told the children of Israel to give to the work of the tabernacle or temple and made the stipulation for them to give. The stipulation was that they had to want to give willingly in order to be part of God's work. So, Jesus doesn't force anyone to believe, He offered His own life freely and willing so others would have the chance and choice to choose him. Now, the bible is clear those who believe and are baptized shall be saved, but those who believe not shall be damned.

A bloody queen was determined to put a stop to the Reformation momentum in England which had begun during her father's rule. She had hundreds of Protestants killed which led to an exodus to the Americas. This is the historic base for people taking sail to America for freedom to worship God the Father and His Son Jesus Christ as declared in truth in the Holy Bible. This is a fundamental fact to remember when you consider the Mayflower Compact which is considered to be one of the first governing documents to shape our nations principles, laws, values, ideologies, and education of our children.

The Mayflower Compact

In the name of God, Amen. We, whose names are underwritten, the loyal subjects of our dread Sovereigne Lord, King James, by the grace of God, of Great Britaine, France and Ireland king, defender of the faith, etc. having undertaken, **for the glory of God**, and **advancement of the Christian faith,** and honour of our king and country, a voyage to plant the first colony in the Northerne parts of Virginia, doe by these presents solemnly and mutually in the presence of God and one of another, covenant and combine ourselves together into a civil body politick, for our better ordering and preservation, and furtherance of the ends aforesaid; and by virtue hereof to enact, constitute, and frame such just and equal laws, ordinances, acts, constitutions and offices, from time to time, as shall be thought most meete and convenient for the general good of the Colonie unto which we promise all due submission and obedience. In witness whereof we have hereunder subscribed our names at Cape-Codd the 11. of November, in the year of the raigne of our sovereigne lord, King James, of England, France and Ireland, the eighteenth, and of Scotland the fiftie-fourth. Anno Dom. 1620.

The advancement of the Christian faith phrase is the central focus of the purpose and plan of government in the new land we now call America. So the Roots of the Unites States from the reformation by Protestant Christians to return to the Bible for answers and solutions to early puritan heritage established our nation upon the faith of Jesus Christ as based upon the teachings of Jesus and verified by the Holy Scriptures. This is a vital truth to know and understand why and how America became a great nation and the dire consequences of allowing the Godly heritage and foundations of our nation to be chipped away.

The truth is that true undefiled religion is to visit the fatherless and the widows in their affliction. This is what scripture teaches is true and undefiled religion. Today the word religion is thrown around as to include anybody's personal subjective believe of any deity their mind could concoct. The Bible is clear about true and undefiled. This is an important principle because many people in this nation and others may not fully understand the history of our nation's faith.

In other words, religion is used when people talk about the first amendment as if religion was every believe system throughout all the continents of the earth is what freedom of religion means or they feel that is what the constitution meant. This is so far from the truth; it is sad; so many people have been misled over such a short period of time considering the youth of our nation compared to that of other nations. Freedom of religion from our nations Foundations is not every religion thrown into a hat to cater too. The opposite is true in the sense of our nations Christian Judaeo values and laws and ethics and morals. This is clear by the Ten Commandments engraved into the walls of the Supreme Court. The Ten Commandments were given by God to Moses in the holy mount to guide His holy people the children of Israel, God's chosen people, and is a strong bond between America and Israel.

In fact, the Bible teaches Christians should love and show compassion and mercy on God's chosen people, the Jewish people, because we were grafted into the vine and we were an unnatural branch but the Jewish people can be grafted back into the vine because they are the natural branches and by Jesus Christ and faith in Him as the only begotten Son of God we can be grafted into Gods kingdom. So, we have been adopted into the family of God through Jesus Christ. This being said the Ten Commandments teach thou shalt have no other God before me. In other words, God is a jealous God and there is none other God but Him even though there be called god and lords many in the world. Christians know there is only one God who created the heaven and the earth the sea and all that dwell there in. The biblical account is so clear in Genesis that the great God of heaven made man in His own image and likeness.

HE WHO WAS

Prophetic Reliability

The Great I Am has prepared history to reveal his glory and two major prophetic assurances fulfilled allow us to see God's hand and preeminence in time and events. The bible speaks of time and chance as well as His eternal control displayed through reliable Prophetic events. These occurrences allow us to understand that we are not just mistakes making mishaps, but that He loves us and has a divine good purpose and will for our lives if we submit our will to Him. Clearly, Joseph and Esther reveal the Lord's divine interventions to protect and care for His people.

The prophetic time line God gave to Abraham generations before they happened also shows times are in His hand. For instance, God revealed to Abraham that his descendants would serve in bondage for four hundred years. Remarkably, the children of Israel departed from Egypt on the exact day as was proclaimed generations earlier. God even revealed to Abraham that his seed would return in the fourth generation "…for the iniquity of the Amorites is not yet full (Genesis 15: partial 16, KJV)." This is a clue to the timeline for us in the last days as Daniel shares a similar phrase "…when the transgressors are come to the full (Daniel 8: partial 23, KJV)." This prophetic evidence from the past was fulfilled over four hundred years to the exact day, so when we see good called evil and evil good we know the closer to that day on the timeline the train of destiny has gone.

The second occurrence takes place in the times of the kings of Israel and an evil king named Jeroboam caused Israel to sin a very grievous and wicked sin. The sin involved setting up polluted altars in Samaria for fear the people would return to Jerusalem to sacrifice at the temple and return to allegiance with Judah. God had stripped eleven of the twelve tribes from Solomon for allowing his strange wives to set up idols. God left Solomon with the tribe of Judah for the promise He made to David his father concerning his seed. This is comforting to believers who have prayed and prayed for God to have mercy upon their children, that God even after their passing remembered the promise he made them. All live unto Him, for He is not a God of the dead but of the living for all live unto Him.

This set up a show down with the kingdom of Israel and the kingdom of Judah which would last between many kings and generations. This also set up a reckoning from the Almighty toward the evils and confusion happening in Samaria. The Lord decided to send a young prophet from Judah to Bethel: and Jeroboam stood by the altar to burn incense.

"And he cried against the altar in the word of the LORD, and said, O altar, altar, thus saith the LORD; Behold, a child shall be born unto the house of David, Josiah by name; and upon thee shall he offer the priests of the high places that burn incense upon thee, and men's bones shall be burnt upon thee (I kings 13:2, KJV).

The incredibly amazing feature of this historic prophetic event was the fact that God revealed to the young prophet and to the people the actual name of the king of Judah who would cleanse and restore righteousness to the nation. Furthermore, King Josiah would not even be born until around thirteen generations of kings in Judah later which is equally fascinating. In other words, the very day Josiah went to Samaria to enforce a nationwide effort to restore the law of God in Israel and to remove every offensive thing in the sight of the Almighty God of Jacob. Josiah saw the grave of the young prophet which was buried close by where he had prophesied some thirteen generations early. Josiah took note while burning the bones of the idolatrous prophets on the same altar, just as was said he would do.

2 Kings Chapter 23:

1.) *And the king sent, and they gathered unto him all the elders of Judah and of Jerusalem.*

2.) *And the king went up into the house of the LORD, and all the men of Judah and all the inhabitants of Jerusalem with him, and the priests, and the prophets, and all the people, both small and great: and he read in their ears all the words of the book of the covenant which was found in the house of the LORD.*

3.) *And the king stood by a pillar, and made a covenant before the LORD, to walk after the LORD, and to keep his commandments and his testimonies and his statutes with all their heart and all their soul, to perform the words of this covenant that were written in this book. And all the people stood to the covenant.*

4.) And the king commanded Hilkiah the high priest, and the priests of the second order, and the keepers of the door, to bring forth out of the temple of the LORD all the vessels that were made for Baal, and for the grove, and for all the host of heaven: and he burned them without Jerusalem in the fields of Kidron, and carried the ashes of them unto Bethel.

5.) And he put down the idolatrous priests, whom the kings of Judah had ordained to burn incense in the high places in the cities of Judah, and in the places round about Jerusalem; them also that burned incense unto Baal, to the sun, and to the moon, and to the planets, and to all the host of heaven.

6.) And he brought out the grove from the house of the LORD, without Jerusalem, unto the brook Kidron, and burned it at the brook Kidron, and stamped it small to powder, and cast the powder thereof upon the graves of the children of the people.

7.) And he broke down the houses of the sodomites, that were by the house of the LORD, where the women wove hangings for the grove.

8.) And he brought all the priests out of the cities of Judah, and defiled the high places where the priests had burned incense, from Geba to Beersheba, and brake down the high places of the gates that were in the entering in of the gate of Joshua the governor of the city, which were on a man's left hand at the gate of the city.

9.) Nevertheless, the priests of the high places came not up to the altar of the LORD in Jerusalem, but they did eat of the unleavened bread among their brethren.

10.) And he defiled Topheth, which is in the valley of the children of Hinnom, that no man might make his son or his daughter to pass through the fire to Molech.

11.) And he took away the horses that the kings of Judah had given to the sun, at the entering in of the house of the LORD, by the chamber of Nathanmelech the chamberlain, which was in the suburbs, and burned the chariots of the sun with fire.

12.) And the altars that were on the top of the upper chamber of Ahaz, which the kings of Judah had made, and the altars which Manasseh had made in the two courts of the house of the LORD, did the king beat down, and brake them down from thence, and cast the dust of them into the brook Kidron.

13.) And the high places that were before Jerusalem, which were on the right hand of the mount of corruption, which Solomon the king of Israel had builded for Ashtoreth the abomination of the Zidonians, and for Chemosh the abomination of the Moabites, and for Milcom the abomination of the children of Ammon, did the king defile.

14.) And he brake in pieces the images, and cut down the groves, and filled their places with the bones of men.

15.) Moreover, the altar that was at Bethel, and the high place which Jeroboam the son of Nebat, who made Israel to sin, had made, both that altar and the high place he brake down, and burned the high place, and stamped it small to powder, and burned the grove.

16.) And as Josiah turned himself, he spied the sepulchres that were there in the mount, and sent, and took the bones out of the sepulchres, and burned them upon the altar, and polluted it, according to the word of the LORD which the man of God proclaimed, who proclaimed these words.

17.) Then he said, What title is that that I see? And the men of the city told him, It is the sepulchre of the man of God, which came from Judah, and proclaimed these things that thou hast done against the altar of Bethel.

18.) And he said, Let him alone; let no man move his bones. So they let his bones alone, with the bones of the prophet that came out of Samaria.

19.) And all the houses also of the high places that were in the cities of Samaria, which the kings of Israel had made to provoke the LORD to anger, Josiah took away, and did to them according to all the acts that he had done in Bethel.

20.) And he slew all the priests of the high places that were there upon the altars, and burned men's bones upon them, and returned to Jerusalem.

21.) And the king commanded all the people, saying, Keep the passover unto the LORD your God, as it is written in the book of this covenant.

22.) Surely there was not holden such a passover from the days of the judges that judged Israel, nor in all the days of the kings of Israel, nor of the kings of Judah;

23.) But in the eighteenth year of king Josiah, wherein this passover was holden to the LORD in Jerusalem.

24.) Moreover, the workers with familiar spirits, and the wizards, and the images, and the idols, and all the abominations that were spied in the land of Judah and in Jerusalem, did Josiah put away, that he might perform the words of the law which were written in the book that Hilkiah the priest found in the house of the LORD.

25.) And like unto him was there no king before him, that turned to the LORD with all his heart, and with all his soul, and with all his might, according to all the law of Moses; neither after him arose there any like him.

This is especially moving considering how a similar King Jesus was prophesied to appear almost the same number of generations apart as Josiah. In fact, the book of Isaiah, which was around three generations of kings prior to the Babylonian captivity, delivers the prophecy God gave Isaiah concerning a sign. The sign is given in Isaiah 7:14 as follows.

Therefore, the Lord himself shall give you a sign; Behold, a virgin shall conceive, and bear a son, and shall call his name Immanuel.

Gods' Stamp of Approval

Now to leave the shallow water and launch out into deeper waters of the mystery of God's plan to redeem man unfolds extraordinarily through the Virgin Mary with great precision in terms of the historic timeline and significance.

Matthew 1:17
So all the generations from Abraham to David are fourteen generations; and from David until the carrying away into Babylon are fourteen generations; **and from the carrying away into Babylon unto Christ are fourteen generations.**

This explosive timeline helps us to realize the Master's hand is ever guiding. The unveiling of God in the flesh was manifested, and Matthew recorded the good news of Jesus Christ the Son of God into the world in the gospel:

Matthew 1:23
Behold, a virgin shall be with child, and shall bring forth a son, and they shall call his name Emmanuel, which being interpreted is, God with us.

Acts 2:23&24
Him, being delivered by the determinate counsel and foreknowledge of God, ye have taken, and by wicked hands have crucified and slain:

Whom God hath raised up, having loosed the pains of death: because it was not possible that he should be holden of it.

The incredible connection between God and His friend Abraham has vastly valuable significance within layers and depths of purposes and meaning through the proving of Abraham's faith. The first layer of the divine blessing of God upon Abraham started with the calling for him to leave his father's house and go to a land that the Lord would give him for an inheritance. This calling involves a natural and spiritual component that required Abraham to trust God with his life and family. The calling required an action of faith to receive the promise of God. This picture of God's calling of Abraham very much parallels Jesus' calling the disciples, some who were fishermen, to leave their fishing business to follow the Savior. The same way the call today for people to repent and believe that Jesus is the Son of God requires trust and faith in God to turn their life's over to the great and merciful high priest.

Genesis 12

1.) *Now the LORD had said unto Abram, Get thee out of thy country, and from thy kindred, and from thy father's house, unto a land that I will shew thee:*

2.) *And I will make of thee a great nation, and I will bless thee, and make thy name great; and thou shalt be a blessing:*

3.) *And I will bless them that bless thee, and curse him that curseth thee: and in thee shall all families of the earth be blessed.*

4.) *So Abram departed, as the LORD had spoken unto him; and Lot went with him: and Abram was seventy and five years old when he departed out of Haran.*

5.) *And Abram took Sarai his wife, and Lot his brother's son, and all their substance that they had gathered, and the souls that they had gotten in Haran; and they went forth to go into the land of Canaan; and into the land of Canaan they came.*

6.) *And Abram passed through the land unto the place of Sichem, unto the plain of Moreh. And the Canaanite was then in the land.*

7.) *And the LORD appeared unto Abram, and said, Unto thy seed will I give this land: and there builded he an altar unto the LORD, who appeared unto him.*

The calling was also comprised with a reward of inheritance. An inheritance and reward which was possibly the land he would be going to. So, Abram obeyed by faith to venture toward the land he would be shown. Interestingly, Abram's step of faith led to God revealing even more of the plan to him, as he learned next that his seed would inherit the land. The spiritual component of the promise was also activated in this step of faith that would affect all the families of the earth being blessed. Wow, how soon would this happen, how patient would Abram have to be, how would the plan that God had for him work out? The spiritual component also involved land. However, a good spiritual country and a new heaven and a new earth wherein dwelleth righteousness are revealed in

Hebrews
Chapter 11:

14.) For they that say such things declare plainly that they seek a country.

15.) And truly, if they had been mindful of that country from whence they came out, they might have had opportunity to have returned.

16.) But now they desire a better country, that is, an heavenly: wherefore God is not ashamed to be called their God: for he hath prepared for them a city.

Knowledge of the Truth

This journey with the Master was initiated by faith but soon an even deeper revelation would be manifested. The truth is, sometimes we think we are in control of our lives, or somehow in the monotonous passing of days, weeks, months, years, and decades we soon begin to wonder will anything change to the way we want it to be, or are we stuck in a cycle of repetition and trapped in certain circumstances. We will soon see the truth that God's plan was far greater than Abraham could have ever imagined even though his patience would be tempered over many years of waiting for the same promise. Abram and Sarai were without a child and heir. However, God had an immaculate plan designed to bring about His perfect will.

The perfect will of God is so coveted to be found of the Lord to whom a day is as thousand years and a thousand years as one day. Therefore, if a person seeks Him and draws nigh unto Him, the scripture is very clear the Lord will draw nigh to them. This is a beautiful promise and shew of God's everlasting love to those who can make many mistakes along the way, or choose their own way, or are so influenced by other people to whom they conform their identity to make themselves somehow pleasing or acceptable in the eyes of others, instead of the one in whose image they are made. This is the amazing grace of God like the song declares when we've been there ten thousand years bright shining as the sun. Imagine such splendor and such peace and comfort of love on the day the promise we have waited for so long is finally here, a reality, and see the face of the Lord Jesus himself who saved us and loved us and knew us well before we ever knew Him. Oh, what a glorious day that will be when Jesus we shall see, when we look upon His face, the one who saved us by His grace, what a day that will be.

God was working a divine Masterpiece through the life of a man named Abram and a holy woman of faith named Sarai. The relationship and communication between God and Abram was so special. The relationship we read about in the bible gives us the divine view as God leads Abram and Abram prays and worships God in spirit and in truth. Yes, Abraham questioned God's plan as time in his perspective probably seemed like it was running out of the hourglass while he waited. Nevertheless, they trusted God with their lives as the author and finisher of their faith because He had started them on this journey of faith to begin with. They also had lots of other activities in their lives, as the Lord taught; "occupy till I come." Abram had great wealth and power while he waited, along with a group of trained men ready for war if necessary. This is seen in Genesis when the city of Sodom, where his nephew Lot lived was overthrown and carried captive by a band of kings from a foreign land. Abram took trained soldiers by night and attacked the enemy army and delivered the city from the hand of its captors.

Great is our Lord, and of great power; His understanding is infinite (KJV, Ps. 147:5). God's scope of understanding is infinite in time and events of history before, during, and after they happen. This is also shown in a vision like experience he had with the Lord while offering sacrifices. Astonishingly, the Lord's infinite understanding provided a key detail to Abraham about his children. Specifically, Abraham was told about the horrible bondage that awaited his descendants three to four generations in the future. Abraham was actually told about the times of his one day grandson Jacob who would become a great nation of people. God's chosen and holy people are the children of Israel. The details are provided in Genesis fifteen as follows.

Genesis 15

6.) And he believed in the LORD; and he counted it to him for righteousness.

7.) And he said unto him, I am the LORD that brought thee out of Ur of the Chaldees, to give thee this land to inherit it.

8.) And he said, Lord GOD, whereby shall I know that I shall inherit it?

9.) And he said unto him, Take me an heifer of three years old, and a she goat of three years old, and a ram of three years old, and a turtledove, and a young pigeon.

10.) And he took unto him all these, and divided them in the midst, and laid each piece one against another: but the birds divided he not.

11.) And when the fowls came down upon the carcases, Abram drove them away.

12.) And when the sun was going down, a deep sleep fell upon Abram; and, lo, an horror of great darkness fell upon him.

13.) And he said unto Abram, Know of a surety that thy seed shall be a stranger in a land that is not theirs, and shall serve them; and they shall afflict them four hundred years;

14.) And also that nation, whom they shall serve, will I judge: and afterward shall they come out with great substance.

15.) And thou shalt go to thy fathers in peace; thou shalt be buried in a good old age.

16.) But in the fourth generation they shall come hither again: for the iniquity of the Amorites is not yet full.

17.) And it came to pass, that, when the sun went down, and it was dark, behold a smoking furnace, and a burning lamp that passed between those pieces.

The children of Israel's journey into Egyptian bondage and departing exodus after four hundred years are described before they existed in versus thirteen and fourteen. Furthermore, the focus of verse sixteen is an integral component for us today as it is a clue which when placed in the continuum comparison with a scripture in the book of Daniel will shine the light of understanding on the days and times we are quickly hastening toward today. LAMED. Forever, O LORD, thy word is settled in heaven (KJV, Ps. 119:89). The message God gave to Abraham is one of the clues to the fulfillment of the finishing moments of world history which involves the timing of the judgment of God. Romans 11: 33 declare "O the depth of the riches both of the wisdom and knowledge of God! How unsearchable are his judgments, and his ways past finding out!"

Timeline of Righteousness and Judgment

Specifically, Abraham was given the reason for his descendants having to wait four generations to return to the promise land, Canaan. The reason was due to the fact the iniquity of the Amorites was not yet full. In other words, God could not transition the land into His people's possession until the iniquity of the people of the land was so evil the judgment of God required their destruction or the Lord was giving room or time for repentance like He gave Jezebel room to repent. Ironically, the missing piece to the puzzle would be well after the people had inherited the land. In fact, the children of Israel over many generations had sinned so grievously before God in their promised land they were taken captive by the Babylonian Kingdom. The Lord had warned His chosen ones not to commit the sins of Idolatry as the nations who God had destroyed before them, but they refused to heed the warning. Over and over they rejected the Word of the Lord to turn from their sins.

The bible often speaks of a remnant that would be saved. A remnant is a small group of believers who had trusted God when the leaders or majority had drifted down a wrong path that led to destruction of the innocent and thus angering a loving and merciful God. For instance, the prophet Jeremiah had spoken to the people by the leading of the Holy Spirit to submit to the Babylonians so they could have peace during their captivity which would last seventy years, and then they would return to their homeland. However, the king was afraid of the Jewish people already in captivity mocking him so he refused to listen.

Jeremiah was so faithful he kept telling the people and the king and counselors the truth even though false prophets prophesied lies to the people. Jeremiah was at one point imprisoned when military leaders sought for his arrest, charging him with lowering the morale of the troops. Nevertheless, Jeremiah cried out to the Lord because he was made a reproach by the people not wanting to hear or obey God's truth and direction and correction. Amazingly, the Lord did exactly what he had spoken through the prophet Jeremiah, as the king was captured for not submitting, and eyes plucked out after they killed his sons the princes. The city was ravished by the invading army, but miraculously Jeremiah was allowed to stay in Jerusalem with a remnant of other people by the Babylonian leaders.

God protected Jeremiah as he had promised him even though much of the entire nation had turned against him, but more accurately the nation had turned against their God that gave them the land. Jonah 2: 8 describes the result of forsaking God and turning to lying vanities: "They that observe lying vanities forsake their own mercy." This is a relevant point illustrated in a relevant book of the bible by a relevant prophet who understood God's mercy, but wasn't obedient at the onset to follow it through until he himself needed the same mercy extended to him again. Jonah was a prophet who was told to go to Nineveh the great city.

Jonah 1: 1-3

1.) Now the word of the LORD came unto Jonah the son of Amittai, saying,

2.) Arise, go to Nineveh, that great city, and cry against it; for their wickedness is come up before me.

3.) But Jonah rose up to flee unto Tarshish from the presence of the LORD, and went down to Joppa; and he found a ship going to Tarshish: so he paid the fare thereof, and went down into it, to go with them unto Tarshish from the presence of the LORD.

Distinctly important to note is the phrase ...for their wickedness is come up before me, and is similar to the phrase before God destroyed Sodom and Gomorrah. God had a message for Abraham His friend and went to visit him and took two angels with Him. A mystery concerning this passage is how Abraham knew it was God and two angels in the form of men. Notice the term men not human as the term human was coined around the eighteen hundred and refers to people as ape people or through a secular humanistic world view even though many may not even realize its origin when they use the term. God revealed something wonderfully personal to Abraham that he had waited for so many years to hear. However, God also had another mission on earth to discover if the sin of Sodom and Gomorrah was as evil as He had heard.

Genesis 18: 20-21

And the LORD said, because the cry of Sodom and Gomorrah is great, and because their sin is very grievous;

I will go down now, and see whether they have done altogether according to the cry of it, which is come unto me; and if not, I will know.

So, Jonah is given the phrase ...for their wickedness is come up before me, referring to the city of Nineveh and the judgment of God against it, and Abraham was given the phrase ...the cry of it, which is come unto me; referring to Sodom and Gomorrah. These are telling examples of how sin, evil, and iniquity are progressively destructive; while on the other side is the patient and all-knowing and seeing power of the God of justice and righteousness. The scripture verifies this truth in the New Testament concerning the progressively destructive cycle to death.

James 1:15

Then when lust hath conceived, it bringeth forth sin: and sin, when it is finished, bringeth forth death.

The analogy between the two judgments of God are distinctly unique however, in that in Nineveh's case God's mercy was extending to the people of Nineveh even though a message through Jonah of the utter destruction of the city within a matter of days had been declared. The main distinction between the two events was the response of the people of the city. The king of Nineveh humbled himself when he heard the judgment of God upon their city had been pronounced. Furthermore, he proclaimed to the people to humble themselves because God may turn from His wrath and spare the city, and that's exactly what happened to the discouragement of Jonah.

God eventually explained to Jonah the reason He had mercy upon the city when the people and the leaders turned for forgiveness. One of the reasons God spared the city when they humbled themselves seeking mercy was due to the fact the people could not discern their right hand from their left hand. The people of Nineveh were so filled with a lack of discernment between good and evil that they were likely ignorant of their own wickedness, or that their actions were considered wicked before a just and holy God. Although, their swift repentance at the preaching of Jonah may also be a hint that the people realized how far morally they had fallen and needed help.

The cities of Sodom and Gomorrah were a stark contrast in their response to the judgment lurking close to them. The two angels sent by God to examine the city quickly found themselves rescuing Abraham's nephew Lot from the men of the city. The people of Sodom had given themselves over to fornication to the point of trying to get to the men or angels who had entered the city in order to "know" them, or actually rape them even after the angels had blinded the evil assembly of wicked doers and pulled Lot into the house and closed the door. They were so evil they were blinded and could not see yet still tried to grope around and find the door. The angels told Lot with haste to try and get any family prepared to leave the city because the next day fire would destroy the city.

Finally, the second part of the mystery concerning flashes of God's righteous judgment in the past and the alignment of Old Testament judgments with prophesies regarding the end times as provided through the prophet Daniel. Daniel was given gifts to interpret dreams and understand mysteries and was beloved by God, protected in the lions' den while being considered one of the wisest men of God in history. Daniel was taken as a youngster by the Babylonian authority and became the presiding presidential leader of one of the most powerful kingdoms of all time. Nebuchadnezzar had a dream that troubled him so he called all the magicians, astrologers, and wise men of the kingdom to interpret the dream with no avail.

The task of interpreting the dream was also magnified when the king couldn't remember the dream and accused the wise men of attempting to gain extra time till the matter was past. So, he demanded all the wise men be destroyed. Daniel and his three Hebrew companions asked God to reveal to them the dream. Faithfully, God revealed the dream and interpretation that very night so they rushed him into the presence of the king. The dream involved a huge statue with a head of gold which Daniel explained God revealed to be the current kingdom. Also, the bible teaches the interpretation of the dream went even further by transcending through the dominant kingdoms of time. The conclusion of the dream reveals that the last kingdom will be an everlasting kingdom and dominion. Directly referring to the kingdom of God and His Son Jesus Christ who will rule and reign forever.

This was a prelude in the life of Daniel to more visions and revelations concerning the last days. A jewel within the mysteries of God's kingdom and timing throughout history is brought to light in the following scripture:

Daniel 8:23
And in the latter time of their kingdom, when the transgressors are come to the full, a king of fierce countenance, and understanding dark sentences, shall stand up.

The connection between "for the iniquity of the Amorites is not yet full" revealed by God to Abraham His friend and "in the latter time of their kingdom, when the transgressors are come to the full," revealed by God unto His beloved Daniel is a clear indicator that God knows exactly the state of men, cities, nations, and the world. Therefore, God's righteous judgment waits till either the sin of men has spread so vastly and fully unto utter destruction or until the precious fruit of the earth has been prepared for His return.

2 Peter 3: 2-15

> *2.) That ye may be mindful of the words which were spoken before by the holy prophets, and of the commandment of us the apostles of the Lord and Saviour:*
>
> *3.) Knowing this first, that there shall come in the last days scoffers, walking after their own lusts,*
>
> *4.) And saying, Where is the promise of his coming? for since the fathers fell asleep, all things continue as they were from the beginning of the creation.*
>
> *5.) For this they willingly are ignorant of, that by the word of God the heavens were of old, and the earth standing out of the water and in the water:*
>
> *6.) Whereby the world that then was, being overflowed with water, perished:*
>
> *7.) But the heavens and the earth, which are now, by the same word are kept in store, reserved unto fire against the day of judgment and perdition of ungodly men.*
>
> *8.) But, beloved, be not ignorant of this one thing, that one day is with the Lord as a thousand years, and a thousand years as one day.*
>
> *9.) The Lord is not slack concerning his promise, as some men count slackness; but is longsuffering to us-ward, not willing that any should perish, but that all should come to repentance.*
>
> *10.) But the day of the Lord will come as a thief in the night; in the which the heavens shall pass away with a great noise, and the elements shall melt with fervent heat, the earth also and the works that are therein shall be burned up.*
>
> *11.) Seeing then that all these things shall be dissolved, what manner of persons ought ye to be in all holy conversation and godliness,*
>
> *12.) Looking for and hasting unto the coming of the day of God, wherein the heavens being on fire shall be dissolved, and the elements shall melt with fervent heat?*
>
> *13.) Nevertheless we, according to his promise, look for new heavens and a new earth, wherein dwelleth righteousness.*
>
> *14.) Wherefore, beloved, seeing that ye look for such things, be diligent that ye may be found of him in peace, without spot, and blameless.*
>
> *15.) And account that the longsuffering of our Lord is salvation; even as our beloved brother Paul also according to the wisdom given unto him hath written unto you;*

Jesus was the word made flesh, and the scripture says His words are Spirit and they are life. How wonderful it is to know when His word is mixed with faith it releases incredible potential for someone to believe the truth and to know the truth, and the truth to make them free. Jesus often encouraged His followers to believe. The bible declares without faith it is impossible to please God for we must believe that He is and that He is a rewarder of them that diligently seek Him. This brings us to a transition necessary to discover the fruit of true transforming faith. John the Baptist exclaimed; bring forth fruit worthy of repentance. In other words let your life produce good works so that you're repenting is known to be sincere.

The Lord offers salvation as a free gift, by grace ye are saved through faith and that not of yourselves it is the gift of God. The bible teaches that by His mercy He saved us. Amazing love how can this be, that He my king should die for me the song says. The testimony of Jesus is the Spirit of prophecy because He which is, and which was, and which is to come promised if He went away He would prepare a place for us, that where He is we may be also. His love was and is so great He laid down His own life for those who couldn't save themselves.

A potentially fearful part of the Holy Scriptures describes a time we may be experiencing at some degree now. A time when God has extended His love toward men and women, cities and nations, and some have received His love and some have rejected that love which could save their souls. It is a fearful thing to fall into the hands of the living God. This is especially the concerning case about people being on the precipice of the final judgments of God upon evil doers.

2 Thessalonians 2:3-14

3.) Let no man deceive you by any means: for that day shall not come, except there come a falling away first, and that man of sin be revealed, the son of perdition;

4.) Who opposeth and exalteth himself above all that is called God, or that is worshipped; so that he as God sitteth in the temple of God, shewing himself that he is God.

5.) Remember ye not, that, when I was yet with you, I told you these things?

6.) And now ye know what withholdeth that he might be revealed in his time.

7.) For the mystery of iniquity doth already work: only he who now letteth will let, until he be taken out of the way.

8.) And then shall that Wicked be revealed, whom the Lord shall consume with the spirit of his mouth, and shall destroy with the brightness of his coming:

9.) Even him, whose coming is after the working of Satan with all power and signs and lying wonders,

10.) And with all deceivableness of unrighteousness in them that perish; because they received not the love of the truth, that they might be saved.

11.) And for this cause God shall send them strong delusion, that they should believe a lie:

12.) That they all might be damned who believed not the truth, but had pleasure in unrighteousness.

13.) But we are bound to give thanks alway to God for you, brethren beloved of the Lord, because God hath from the beginning chosen you to salvation through sanctification of the Spirit and belief of the truth:

14.) Whereunto he called you by our gospel, to the obtaining of the glory of our Lord Jesus Christ.

Think closely about the phrase above in verse ten "because they received not the love of the truth, that they might be saved." So, the cause of God's wrath after the falling away is clearly stated in the fact that some received not the love of the truth. Interestingly, freedom comes from the truth as described in the Word of God as; know the truth and the truth shall make you free. Deceitful evil pleasures seem to allure through the lust of the flesh as though they will bring satisfaction and freedom by removing any sense of self-restraint. However, the problem with lustful pleasures of the flesh and mind is they are shallow and short lived. As a matter of fact, the bible teaches sin brings a man low. It also teaches that people are actually in bondage to sin rather than being free. The scripture also provides the source of the temptation and bondage to sin. It teaches some people are taken captive by the enemy at his own will. Of course, the enemy is the devil and the bible calls him the god of this world.

For instance, the devil is exposed early on in Genesis when he deceives Adam and Eve. The scripture describes him as the most subtle of the beasts. The wicked one lured Eve into his web with partial truths which led to lies that were deceptively spun to reach his final goal of killing Adam and Eve, or better yet in this case causing them to eventually bring death upon themselves and consequently all of mankind. The devil came but for to kill, steal, and destroy. Jesus came that we might have life and have it more abundantly. Therefore, we can explore the beginnings of the enemy in order to learn more about how he operates and why.

The book of Ezekiel describes Lucifer the son of the morning as a created being by God almighty as the anointed Cherub that covereth. This snake of a beast was cast down because the bible says pride was found in his heart when once he was so beautiful with instruments built into him to worship the true and living God. The immense beauty corrupted the bright creature as he wanted to sit in the seat of God. Amongst the stones of fire he walked in the holy mountain of God, and in his great fall he drew a third of the angels with him. Now some are chained in everlasting chains under darkness until the great Day of Judgment.

The enemy is seen being cast down but his initial motive to sit in the seat of God will remain and be manifested through a vile man who he empowers to call and exalt himself above everything that is called God. So, the start of his encounters with man started with the woman. One of the first fiery darts he threw her way was hath God said? He cast doubt in her mind about what she knew God actually told Adam. The three principles of lust were introduced to Eve that day and the three are still being utilized today. She saw the tree was good for food, lust of the flesh because they were told not to eat of the tree of good and evil. This may be why the bible teaches if we regard iniquity He will not hear our prayers, and that we should cast down imaginations and every high thing that exalts itself against the knowledge of God.

Notice unlike modern depictions, the tree was likely not an apple tree. The fruit was a spiritual fruit as Adam and Eve were natural and spiritual people in a spiritual and natural garden because they were told they could eat of all the fruit trees in the garden except the one tree of knowledge of good and evil. God made man of the dust and breathed into man and man became a living soul. Why does the scripture mention people believing the testimony God gave of His Son Jesus to the saving of the soul by the knowledge of the truth of the good news of the Gospel? The bible teaches God chose the foolishness of preaching to save the lost because the foolishness of God is wiser than man.

I Corinthians 1:18-31

18.) For the preaching of the cross is to them that perish foolishness; but unto us which are saved it is the power of God.

19.) For it is written, I will destroy the wisdom of the wise, and will bring to nothing the understanding of the prudent.

20.) Where is the wise? where is the scribe? where is the disputer of this world? hath not God made foolish the wisdom of this world?

21.) For after that in the wisdom of God the world by wisdom knew not God, it pleased God by the foolishness of preaching to save them that believe.

22.) For the Jews require a sign, and the Greeks seek after wisdom:

23.) But we preach Christ crucified, unto the Jews a stumblingblock, and unto the Greeks foolishness;

24.) But unto them which are called, both Jews and Greeks, Christ the power of God, and the wisdom of God.

25.) Because the foolishness of God is wiser than men; and the weakness of God is stronger than men.

26.) For ye see your calling, brethren, how that not many wise men after the flesh, not many mighty, not many noble, are called:

27.) But God hath chosen the foolish things of the world to confound the wise; and God hath chosen the weak things of the world to confound the things which are mighty;

28 And base things of the world, and things which are despised, hath God chosen, yea, and things which are not, to bring to nought things that are:

29.) That no flesh should glory in his presence.

30.) But of him are ye in Christ Jesus, who of God is made unto us wisdom, and righteousness, and sanctification, and redemption:

31.) That, according as it is written, He that glorieth, let him glory in the Lord.

(Image above: christianitymalaysia.com)

(Image above: <u>thelaymansbiblicalhandbook.com</u>)

Verse nineteen is a reference to an Old Testament statement that opens the eyes of a person's understanding to comprehend the truth that God will destroy the wisdom of the wise, while bringing to nothing the understanding of the prudent. Let's examine these principles in context because the question may be asked concerning wisdom that isn't wisdom a good thing. Surely, a righteous sense of the term would relate to the book of Proverbs where the bible teaches we should cry out for knowledge, wisdom, and understanding. The eternal book also highlights the vital importance and highly valuable reward of attaining the big three, as they are considered more valuable than gold or anything that could be compared to them.

Actually, the scripture discussed two things that bring power and seemingly provide solutions or answers to major issues or concerns of life. Discerning the difference between righteous wisdom and the wisdom of God versus the "wisdom of this world" are actually so vital they can be the difference between life and death, naturally and spiritually. Delving further into this truth requires examining the bases of knowledge and wisdom as revealed by the Holy Scripture as it is in truth the Word of God. The fear of the Lord is the beginning of knowledge. How does everyone have access to the knowledge of God? All men have knowledge the bible declares. The truth speaks through the generations, as the truth of the Lord endureth forever. The truth also takes language to another level of understanding as the heavens His throne and the earth His footstool. His handywork then proves to be so evident it becomes the evidence to the conscience of man that the invisible things of God are clearly seen and understood by His creation.

For the invisible things of him from the creation of the world are clearly seen, being understood by the things that are made, even his eternal power and Godhead; so that they are without excuse (Romans 1:20):

The mystery of God's eternal plan of salvation is revealed through the good news that He sent His only begotten Son into the world to save the world. For God so loved the world, that he gave his only begotten Son, that whosoever believeth in him should not perish, but have everlasting life (John 3:16).

Psalms 19:1-14

1.) *(To the chief Musician, A Psalm of David.) The heavens declare the glory of God; and the firmament sheweth his handywork.*

2.) *Day unto day uttereth speech, and night unto night sheweth knowledge.*

3.) *There is no speech nor language, where their voice is not heard.*

4.) Their line is gone out through all the earth, and their words to the end of the world. In them hath he set a tabernacle for the sun,

5.) Which is as a bridegroom coming out of his chamber, and rejoiceth as a strong man to run a race.

6.) His going forth is from the end of the heaven, and his circuit unto the ends of it: and there is nothing hid from the heat thereof.

7.) The law of the LORD is perfect, converting the soul: the testimony of the LORD is sure, making wise the simple.

8.) The statutes of the LORD are right, rejoicing the heart: the commandment of the LORD is pure, enlightening the eyes.

9.) The fear of the LORD is clean, enduring for ever: the judgments of the LORD are true and righteous altogether.

10.) More to be desired are they than gold, yea, than much fine gold: sweeter also than honey and the honeycomb.

11.) Moreover by them is thy servant warned: and in keeping of them there is great reward.

12.) Who can understand his errors? cleanse thou me from secret faults.

13.) Keep back thy servant also from presumptuous sins; let them not have dominion over me: then shall I be upright, and I shall be innocent from the great transgression.

14.) Let the words of my mouth, and the meditation of my heart, be acceptable in thy sight, O LORD, my strength, and my redeemer.

So, the wisdom of God and Gods thoughts are higher than our thoughts, and His ways are higher than our ways. Therefore, man is wise to seek the wisdom that is from above and not that wisdom which is of this world.

James 3:14-17

14.) But if ye have bitter envying and strife in your hearts, glory not, and lie not against the truth.

15.) This wisdom descendeth not from above, but is earthly, sensual, devilish.

16.) For where envying and strife is, there is confusion and every evil work.

17.) But the wisdom that is from above is first pure, then peaceable, gentle, and easy to be intreated, full of mercy and good fruits, without partiality, and without hypocrisy.

Most certainly, there is a mystery of iniquity and a mystery of righteousness. So, there also are those who walk in the wisdom of God, and some who are wise to do evil. The bible also gives insight to the degrees of true righteousness and wisdom as well as the boundaries of the same. The scripture is clear for a righteous man to have proper balance, rightly dividing the word of truth. In fact, the enemy of every man's soul used, or you may say misused the Holy Scripture in an attempt to pervert the truth in order to make Jesus take the evil bait of temptation to tempt God.

More specifically, the enemy probably tried to even use an ordered attack on Jesus. In other words, the temptation of Jesus in the wilderness actually discusses three different attacks on the Holy One which could have actually been multifaceted. The lure of the first temptation may have been set like a spring to trigger the next one, even if the first was unsuccessful. For example, if the first temptation targeted the armor of God or attempted to weaken the Lord Jesus' spiritual discipline in order to weaken His mind to focus on fleshly lusts, then the old serpent could shoot his next fiery dart unguarded into the life of Christ. The following coercive temptation would likely build on the reverse effect of the first temptation even if, or even because it was unsuccessful.

Distinctly, the result of obedience to God and successful overcoming of a temptation can, if we are not watchful, set the stage for a stage two or tier two temptation. A person's obedience, especially if overcoming the specific temptation involved spiritual sacrifice like fasting and prayer and denying fleshly lustful desires, could potentially make a Christian feel a sense of deep devotion. Absolutely, a sense of deep devotion is a good thing. However, if a believer isn't aware of the boundaries and balance of the truth, the result could cause them to fall for the trap of harming themselves by being over righteous or over wise. The scripture teaches it is good to be zealously effected in a good thing, so zeal is fine, tempting God is not.

Jesus, who is the model of the righteousness of God, as God was in Christ reconciling the world unto Himself, had the discernment to know the difference between what God led Him to do (fasting during the time of those particular temptations) and not turn the rock into bread at the beguiling attempt to cast doubt by the enemy who cast the question of seemingly doubt in the phrase if thou be the Son of God… He also displayed a great lesson of balance for future believers standing by faith against the main three fiery darts of the devil over centuries and ages, which are the lust of the eyes, the lust of the flesh, and the pride of life. Jesus likely had all three darts of the enemy cunningly time-released in what seemed to be consecutive and in strategic order in case Jesus passed one part of the temptation, the devil was prepared and poised to throw the next snare.

So, believers must stand guard against the whiles of the devil in their actions and not give place to the devil. Believers don't need to cast away their confidence which hath great recompense of reward, but they also need to take heed lest they fall. Believers need to take heed to God's Word and rightly divide the Word of truth not being wicked or foolish over much and die before their time, but also not be righteous over much or make themselves over wise and destroy themselves.

Some have said people can't leave the world till God gets ready for them, and in a sense God understands our times, and He also gives us His instruction how to live life and have life and have it more abundantly. For instance, if a person is reckless and rebellious against God's warnings for God is to be feared, the result could be decisions that lead to worse ones that cause them to run their lives over the edge. In an opposing direction, a person could feel so overwhelmingly devoted and dedicated to God but begin to think they have to prove their dedication by their own efforts and not necessarily the leading of the Spirit of God, as many as be led by the Spirit of God are the sons of God, may fall into serious trouble due to a lack of proper balance. Some people have died from fasting.

So fasting is good, however if a person feels their own way of fasting or fair shew in the flesh, or to make themselves look spiritual to receive glory from man, is more important than obedience to God, then what once was obedience in proper fasting to God, could become a snare either way. The enemy could try and influence someone to try a fast too much and cause them to harm themselves, or contrariwise try to make a Christian not take dedication to God seriously enough or too lightly and abuse the things of God for the honor of pleasing or seeking glory of man. Jesus warned against praying to be seen of man in the marketplaces or seeking the best seats in feasts, or making long prayers for pretense seeking the glory of man. The Bible teaches they have their reward. Jesus sought the glory that came from God only that He might please His Father God in heaven and so should we. He exhorts us in His holy Word to go into our closets and close the door and pray and He that sees in secret shall reward us openly.

Finally, the fear of the Lord, wisdom and knowledge of the holy, and righteousness provide a landscape of truth and life. In fact, the scripture clearly outlines the importance of each one both individually and combined below while giving the remedy for staying within the proper balance and the importance of moderation. The scripture also warns of being a stench in the nose of the Almighty by being holier than thou, as we all have sinned and fall short of the glory of God. He does give insight to asking for wisdom for God has no respect of persons and upbraideth not but giveth to all men liberally. However, He warns through the Spirit of God in the holy text to ask for wisdom from God in faith nothing wavering for he that wavereth is like a wave of the sea that is driven with the wind and tossed by every doctrine and the slight of man. So, we must be sure and willing to receive the wisdom that comes from God.

Proverbs 9:10
The **fear of the LORD** *is the beginning of wisdom: and the knowledge of the holy is understanding.*

Proverbs 10:2
Treasures of wickedness profit nothing: but **righteousness** *delivereth from death.*

Ecclesiastes 7:12
For **wisdom** *is a defence, and money is a defence: but the excellency of knowledge is, that wisdom giveth life to them that have it.*

This leads to a really interesting exchange in the book of Isaiah about the importance of the decisions that mankind makes about the knowledge of the Holy One. One scripture concerning the state of man, or even perhaps entire nations describes certain times or a time, or a place, or places when people are faced with making life altering decisions for good or bad, whether to follow God, or the devil, or their own way, "multitudes, multitudes, in the valley of decision." Similarly, the book of Ezekiel goes beyond just the state of making major decisions regarding following the true and living God or following the way of wickedness in the sight of the creator of all living. The New Testament echoes this truth using an analogy between a broad way That leads to destruction and many there be that go through the wide gate, and a narrow way which leadeth unto life through a strait gate.

The assurance of God's Word as absolute truth and absolutely true and inerrant are evidenced through not only time, archaeology, and significant historical findings like the Dead Sea Scrolls and the tomb of Abraham. The history of the disciples as eyewitnesses of Jesus' splendor and love for people are exemplified all the way through his life and ministry of healing the sick, delivering the oppressed from evil spirits, and saying while hanging on a tree between the heaven and earth which He created as He was the Word made flesh, forgive them they know not what they do.

Peter was also one of the eyewitnesses along with John and James who were invited by Jesus to ascend a mountain where His glory would be revealed. The scripture teaches of the miraculous account that Jesus' clothes became incredibly white and shining. The account records Jesus' meeting with two saints from the Old Testament which were Moses and Elijah who represented the law and the prophets. The two major people the Lord chose to lead God's chosen people Israel and the channels He used to guide the people in truth through His laws, commandments, and statutes for future generations after the death of Moses, and the Prophets which revealed God's plans and visions to turn and lead the people in God's righteousness in an ongoing continuum designed for chosen Prophets to fill the room of the old prophets.

These divine offices were instrumental in passing the torch of truth and faith and holiness to the next generation. Therefore, looking back Moses received the Ten Commandments upon the mountain, the prophet Elijah had a great victory over false prophets trying to destroy God's heritage upon a mountain, and then Jesus is standing on the mountain with these two men of God. Jesus, the I Am, was being prepared for what awaited Him in Jerusalem with Peter, James, and John in the midst of this historic encounter. Then, a cloud overshadowed them and a voice said "this is my beloved Son, hear Him." Jesus Christ was the end of the law for righteousness. The law was a school master preparing for the Savior, and the prophet John the Baptist testified that he was not that prophet that should come, but it was revealed to John the Baptist that who he saw the spirit abide upon the same was the

Son of God. This was fulfilled as John was baptizing Jesus in the Jordan River and he saw the Spirit like a dove descend and abide upon.

The disciples that heard the voice were commanded not to tell of the event until after Jesus had risen from the dead. This incredible, miraculous meeting with confirmation from the voice of God the Father from heaven was heard by three witnesses on the scene, as the scripture declares in the mouth of two or three witnesses let every word be established. Astoundingly, Peter declares in the book of Peter that we have a more sure word of prophesy. Holy men spake as they were moved by the Holy Ghost he declares. The holy scripture he concludes is the more sure word of prophesy, even more so than being on the mountain and hearing the voice of God Almighty from the cloud. Another verse of scripture that is astonishing is that He exalts His Word above His name.

This is really fascinating because the bible declares every knee shall bow and every tongue confess that Jesus Christ is Lord to the glory of God the Father. Imagine the return of Jesus Christ in the clouds of glory and the great white throne judgment where small and great will stand before God to be judged for the works they have done in their bodies. The Word of God is quick and powerful and sharper than any two-edged sword dividing asunder of soul and spirit, and is a discerner of the thoughts and intents of the heart. So, God will rightly judge the secrets and intents of men's hearts. So, every knee shall bow and tongue confess that Jesus Christ is Lord and we will be judged by the Words that Jesus spoke. He exalts His

Word above His name. This phrase reminds us that we should not love in tongue or word, but indeed and in truth. The old hand shake where a man's word was his bond because his actions would be backed by his word in faithfulness. One place in the word talks of a faithful man swearing to his own hurt and changing not. The apostle Paul also refers to the power of God's Word when he explained the kingdom is not in word but in Power. In other words, the Word came not with enticing words of man's wisdom but with the demonstration of the Holy Ghost and power. The apostle Paul also told the saints in I Thessalonians that they had received the Word as it was in truth the Word of God.

So, the wonderful assurance of the power and authority of God's Holy Word as the message of God the Father and the Lord Jesus Christ His Son who came in the flesh and gave salvation and offers the gift of the Holy Ghost to as many as obey Him is certain. He who planted the ear can't He hear. So, of course, He can get His message across to the men and women He created and gave understanding to between the womb and the grave. Ezekiel 18 and 33 give the mind of the Lord concerning the righteous and the wicked. God's standard of righteousness as provided through the testimonies of God, His truth.

Ezekiel 33:1-33

1.) Again the word of the LORD came unto me, saying,

2.) Son of man, speak to the children of thy people, and say unto them, When I bring the sword upon a land, if the people of the land take a man of their coasts, and set him for their watchman:

3.) If when he seeth the sword come upon the land, he blows the trumpet, and warn the people;

4.) Then whosoever heareth the sound of the trumpet, and taketh not warning; if the sword come, and take him away, his blood shall be upon his own head.

5.) He heard the sound of the trumpet, and took not warning; his blood shall be upon him. But he that taketh warning shall deliver his soul.

6.) But if the watchman see the sword come, and blow not the trumpet, and the people be not warned; if the sword come, and take any person from among them, he is taken away in his iniquity; but his blood will I require at the watchman's hand.

7.) So thou, O son of man, I have set thee a watchman unto the house of Israel; therefore, thou shalt hear the word at my mouth, and warn them from me.

8.) When I say unto the wicked, O wicked man, thou shalt surely die; if thou dost not speak to warn the wicked from his way, that wicked man shall die in his iniquity; but his blood will I require at thine hand.

9.) Nevertheless, if thou warn the wicked of his way to turn from it; if he does not turn from his way, he shall die in his iniquity; but thou hast delivered thy soul.

10.) Therefore, O thou son of man, speak unto the house of Israel; Thus ye speak, saying, If our transgressions and our sins be upon us, and we pine away in them, how should we then live?

11.) Say unto them, As I live, saith the Lord GOD, I have no pleasure in the death of the wicked; but that the wicked turn from his way and live: turn ye, turn ye from your evil ways; for why will ye die, O house of Israel?

12.) Therefore, thou son of man, say unto the children of thy people, The righteousness of the righteous shall not deliver him in the day of his transgression: as for the wickedness of the wicked, he shall not fall thereby in the day that he turneth from his wickedness; neither shall the righteous be able to live for his righteousness in the day that he sinneth.

13.) When I shall say to the righteous, that he shall surely live; if he trust to his own righteousness, and commit iniquity, all his righteousnesses shall not be remembered; but for his iniquity that he hath committed, he shall die for it.

14.) Again, when I say unto the wicked, Thou shalt surely die; if he turn from his sin, and do that which is lawful and right;

15.) If the wicked restore the pledge, give again that he had robbed, walk in the statutes of life, without committing iniquity; he shall surely live, he shall not die.

16.) None of his sins that he hath committed shall be mentioned unto him: he hath done that which is lawful and right; he shall surely live.

17.) Yet the children of thy people say, The way of the Lord is not equal: but as for them, their way is not equal.

18.) When the righteous turneth from his righteousness, and committeth iniquity, he shall even die thereby.

19.) But if the wicked turn from his wickedness, and do that which is lawful and right, he shall live thereby.

20.) Yet ye say, The way of the Lord is not equal. O ye house of Israel, I will judge you every one after his ways.

21.) And it came to pass in the twelfth year of our captivity, in the tenth month, in the fifth day of the month, that one that had escaped out of Jerusalem came unto me, saying, The city is smitten.

22.) *Now the hand of the LORD was upon me in the evening, afore he that was escaped came; and had opened my mouth, until he came to me in the morning; and my mouth was opened, and I was no more dumb.*

23.) *Then the word of the LORD came unto me, saying,*

24.) *Son of man, they that inhabit those wastes of the land of Israel speak, saying, Abraham was one, and he inherited the land: but we are many; the land is given us for inheritance.*

25.) *Wherefore say unto them, Thus saith the Lord GOD; Ye eat with the blood, and lift up your eyes toward your idols, and shed blood: and shall ye possess the land?*

26.) *Ye stand upon your sword, ye work abomination, and ye defile everyone his neighbour's wife: and shall ye possess the land?*

27.) *Say thou thus unto them, Thus saith the Lord GOD; As I live, surely they that are in the wastes shall fall by the sword, and him that is in the open field will I give to the beasts to be devoured, and they that be in the forts and in the caves shall die of the pestilence.*

28.) *For I will lay the land most desolate, and the pomp of her strength shall cease; and the mountains of Israel shall be desolate, that none shall pass through.*

29.) *Then shall they know that I am the LORD, when I have laid the land most desolate because of all their abominations which they have committed.*

30.) *Also, thou son of man, the children of thy people still are talking against thee by the walls and in the doors of the houses, and speak one to another, everyone to his brother, saying, Come, I pray you, and hear what is the word that cometh forth from the LORD.*

31.) *And they come unto thee as the people cometh, and they sit before thee as my people, and they hear thy words, but they will not do them: for with their mouth they shew much love, but their heart goeth after their covetousness.*

32.) *And, lo, thou art unto them as a very lovely song of one that hath a pleasant voice, and can play well on an instrument: for they hear thy words, but they do them not.*

33.) *and when this cometh to pass, (lo, it will come,) then shall they know that a prophet hath been among them.*

God's instructions to Ezekiel several times through the passages involve a similarly repeated phrase which is "Son of man, speak to the children of thy people, and say unto them," So, God was telling Ezekiel exactly what He wanted Ezekiel to speak to the people. So, the scripture involves God speaking through the prophet the message and information

He wanted to communicate to them. God also relays the evidence that it is in fact He Himself who is the source and sender of the information by telling them when certain judgments take place then they will know. Some may not have believed the prophets words were directed by God and some may have doubted the prophets' accuracy or timing concerning the judgments, but the bible teaches in another place that God is known by the judgment which He executive.

Other scriptures verify the truths of God's voice and instruction to the holy prophets like where it teaches He will do nothing unless He reveal it unto His servants the prophets first. The test of a true prophet in the Old Testament was that the prophet was true if what he proclaimed from the mouth of God happened as He had prophesied from the mouth of God it would. On the contrary, if a prophet prophesied unto the people and it didn't come to pass, the prophet was indeed a false prophet. This test of authenticity of a prophet seems quite simple; however the scripture also teaches because judgment is not executed speedily people continue in sin.

In other words, the judgments of God and the prophecies of the prophets who declare they are speaking the words of God could take time to reach fulfillment. However, some judgments of the Almighty are executed speedily. For example, one Old Testament event involved people disregarding the Word of the Lord given to them by somehow expecting the judgment would take many years to happen. In that particular case, the Word was revealed to the people that it would not be far off as they had thought, but instead the judgement was nigh at hand. Other cases have described situations involving people or leaders or armies, or even nations who feel they are invincible because they have arms on their side, or mighty men, or multitudes on their side. The bible teaches the strength of the horse is a vain thing in the day of battle. Therefore, if God be for you who can be against you the bible declares, but if a person thinks their strength can save them even when they are doing wickedly against his Word, or His commandments or His instruction in Righteousness, the lesson can be very severe. Though hand join in hand they shall not be unpunished.

Proverbs 11:21
Though hand join in hand, the wicked shall not be unpunished: but the seed of the righteous shall be delivered.

Proverbs 16:5
Every one that is proud in heart is an abomination to the LORD: though hand join in hand, he shall not be unpunished.

God's Word is very clear and evidence has been provided regarding some of the methods God sent messages to people through His holy men and women who served Him in truth and sincerity. One place calls His chosen people vessels of honour. It is also worth mentioning the truth and power of God outlines the standards of Righteousness which He has established. This brings us to reckon with the principles of pride, deception, and lies. The scripture clearly gives the source of lies.

The bible declares that satan is a liar and the father of every lie. In further depth, the bible teaches some have not known the depth of satan. Furthermore, the bible teaches if a person lies to someone, they actually hate them. The last verse of Proverbs chapter twenty-six declares the hatred and affliction inflicted by a lying tongue. The twenty fifth verse warns of the deceit of a real hater who is full of deceit. The hater of good may give fair speeches, but seven abominations are in his heart. Sound similar to the scripture which teaches they confess me with their mouth, but their heart is far from me. The Lord Jesus actually told some of His disciples concerning the hypocritical leaders of the day to do what they say but not what they do. In other words, their actions didn't align with their words, yet they were in positions of leadership or supposed to be the learned of the day.

Proverbs 26

1.) *As snow in summer, and as rain in harvest, so honour is not seemly for a fool.*

2.) *As the bird by wandering, as the swallow by flying, so the curse causeless shall not come.*

3.) *A whip for the horse, a bridle for the ass, and a rod for the fool's back.*

4.) *Answer not a fool according to his folly, lest thou also be like unto him.*

5.) *Answer a fool according to his folly, lest he be wise in his own conceit.*

6.) *He that sendeth a message by the hand of a fool cutteth off the feet, and drinketh damage.*

7.) *The legs of the lame are not equal: so is a parable in the mouth of fools.*

8.) *As he that bindeth a stone in a sling, so is he that giveth honour to a fool.*

9.) *As a thorn goeth up into the hand of a drunkard, so is a parable in the mouth of fools.*

10.) *The great God that formed all things both rewardeth the fool, and rewardeth transgressors.*

11.) *As a dog returneth to his vomit, so a fool returneth to his folly.*

12.) *Seest thou a man wise in his own conceit? there is more hope of a fool than of him.*

13.) The slothful man saith, There is a lion in the way; a lion is in the streets.

14.) As the door turneth upon his hinges, so doth the slothful upon his bed.

15.) The slothful hideth his hand in his bosom; it grieveth him to bring it again to his mouth.

16.) The sluggard is wiser in his own conceit than seven men that can render a reason.

17.) He that passeth by, and meddleth with strife belonging not to him, is like one that taketh a dog by the ears.

18.) As a mad man who casteth firebrands, arrows, and death,

19.) So is the man that deceiveth his neighbour, and saith, Am not I in sport?

20.) Where no wood is, there the fire goeth out: so where there is no talebearer, the strife ceaseth.

21.) As coals are to burning coals, and wood to fire; so is a contentious man to kindle strife.

22.) The words of a talebearer are as wounds, and they go down into the innermost parts of the belly.

23.) Burning lips and a wicked heart are like a potsherd covered with silver dross.

24.) He that hateth dissembleth with his lips, and layeth up deceit within him;

25.) When he speaketh fair, believe him not: for there are seven abominations in his heart.

26.) Whose hatred is covered by deceit, his wickedness shall be shewed before the whole congregation.

27.) Whoso diggeth a pit shall fall therein: and he that rolleth a stone, it will return upon him.

28.) A lying tongue hateth those that are afflicted by it; and a flattering mouth worketh ruin.

This is profound truth because it places a visible line of demarcation so to speak between so called gray areas where some may or may not understand the full scope of a situation, or important pieces of the puzzle, like key details which would help to determine the truth of a matter even though all the facts may not yet be revealed. The truth in such cases often has to be searched for and then built upon once information begins to be discovered. Therefore, it may require multiple steps and multiple methods sometimes to find answers to difficult problems or cases.

Oftentimes, criminal cold cases generally involve old crime scenes and old evidence or it likely wouldn't be a cold case. The crime scene and evidence have likely been examined and stored away, thus making age a factor and further complicates the solving of a cold case. However, some cold cases are examined by different investigators who decide to take the journey into retrieving old evidence and even tracking items at the scene in search for new evidence which may have been overlooked. One particular case years ago was solved by tracking the original old television that was at the original crime scene. The likelihood of finding an old television from an apartment that had long been renovated was not very likely especially since it could have been thrown away or completely trashed or even broken if it was somehow found.

Incredibly the old television years after the crime was traced back to whomever it was given or sold to after the crime scene had been investigated. The television was eventually tracked to an old shed where someone had stored it for years and years. Specific clues to uncovering this particular cold case would prove difficult to locate since the crime involved a terrible murder scene cleaned so well with strong chemicals that any hope of finding evidence that the victim had indeed been in the apartment had been exhausted. The criminal had seemingly gotten away with a terrible crime. The one piece of the crime scene the murderer couldn't clean or probably didn't even consider cleaning was the inside parts behind the perforations of the speaker in the old television. This proved to be the seemingly in genius decision to track the old television which was taken apart and the blood evidence of the victim was found which placed the victim in the suspects apartment and thus uncovered the murderer who was finally brought to justice.

This case was an example of how cold cases can be solved and provides an important framework for how truth can be found through diligent search and often in-depth searches which go beyond just surface information. Surface information can sometimes prove misleading depending upon the ideology of the source and purpose of the information. The truth of God's Word is so important because it has the power through the gospel of Jesus Christ to save the soul of man. Many people have vast knowledge in specific fields or subject areas, and many may be expert in their professions or studies. Nevertheless, how important is the soul of a man or woman? The scripture teaches, what does it profit a man if he gain the whole world and lose his own soul, or what can a man give in exchange for his soul? What if a person or medical expert finds a medicine that helps people live healthier and longer like a so-called fountain of youth?

The bible clearly reveals about three times throughout history when God changed the lifespan of man. The first time was around the time of the flood when God informed mans' years would be one hundred and twenty years. Later yet in bible history, the declaration of three score and ten years would be the years of man, and if by reason of strength fourscore years. These are major reductions in the lifespan of man. Especially the first change in lifespan because pre-flood men lived to be almost one thousand years. Methuselah was the oldest recorded man in scripture unless you consider the case of Enoch. Enoch walked with God and was not because God took him because he had this testimony that he pleased God. Elijah was another who was carried up but in a chariot of fire, while Elisha the prophet who filled his room was in attendance.

Then of course, there is the Savior, the Lord Jesus Christ the Son of God in truth who declared no man took His life but He laid it down so our sins and the sins of the whole world could be forgiven. He laid down His life and took it up again because God the Father gave Him the commandment to do so. The scripture also teaches Jesus rose from the dead and became the firstborn from the dead, and that if we believe in Him we also have the hope of the Resurrection. Jesus told Martha before He raised Lazarus her brother from the dead, and after Lazarus had already been dead four days that He was the Resurrection, after she had said that she knew Lazarus would live again in the resurrection.

Another important fact was detailed after Jesus rose from the dead and made known that He had the keys to death, hell, and the grave. The God, who through His Holy Word (Jesus the Word made flesh), created man in His image and in His likeness from the dust and breathed into man and man became a living soul. Surely, man will return unto the dust but where will the soul go. The scripture is clear about two destinations. One destination discussed in scripture refers to paradise where Jesus told the thief beside Him on the cross that "today you will be with Me in paradise" after the thief asked Jesus if He would remember him when He came into His kingdom. What an incredible act of mercy when the Lord Jesus was suffering near the gates of death and in agony.

The second destination discussed in scripture by Jesus Himself is Hell. While, the scripture teaches that hell was not made for man, but was prepared for the devil and his angels. It also makes known men can choose to go there. Almost like the angels who left their first estate are chained under darkness unto the judgment, so men can choose to follow the Old Serpent the devil into hell. However, there is more because the book of Revelation in the New Testament tells of a time when death and hell will be cast into the lake of fire, and that the smoke of their torment will ascend up forever and ever. So, back to the many sources of information, and many people who have knowledge or expertise in specific fields or areas. Even if the vast knowledge was used to help countless multitudes or if the vast knowledge was used to generate evil devises for the Old Testament teaches God made man upright but they sought out many inventions.

Now in light of the multitude of voices and opinions what do you think will really stand the test of time? The scripture declares heaven and earth shall pass away, but the Word of the Lord endureth forever. The bible also teaches He will show whose word will stand, His or those who oppose Him or hate Him. They hated me without a cause, and He came into His own and His own received Him not, other scriptures testify of what happened to Jesus when He came to the earth in the flesh and was born of a virgin. He chose not to come in the form of an angel, but of man through the lineage of Abraham. He was touched with the feeling of our infirmity. He was wounded for our transgressions; He was bruised for our iniquities. Now how important is the knowledge of the truth, His truth in the light that if man lives a total of on average seventy years, where will his eternal soul awake; in paradise with the Lord or in hell where the worm dieth not and the fire is not quenched.

The time frame of the eternal God is His to know as the scripture teaches Jesus doesn't even know the day or the hour, only God the Father. However, the bible clearly details the signs of the times. This is especially of interest to note because the book of Romans in the New Testament was written around two thousand years ago. Why is that so important? The details outlined in the New Testament concerning the signs of the times are so vividly in open view in our present age and are becoming increasingly more exposed seemingly by the day. The dynamics have changed so drastically in our modern time to even compare them to fifty years ago. So, imagine how vastly different the world has become since just one hundred years ago. My granddad was born around 1888 according to the old family bible record which was common to use in that day in case some were born at home and maybe had no birth certificate. An older gentleman once told me at a cookout he remembered my granddad bringing the boys on horse and buggy to town one particular Sunday for haircuts. This really revealed just how different things are compared to what they used to be over just one generation, my granddad's generation. The book of Daniel in the Old Testament prophesied of a time toward the time of the end that knowledge would increase, and people would run to and fro. Amazing considering the time this prophecy was written was probably somewhere around three thousand and four hundred years from this present time.

Well, would that be such a big deal if everything had been the same as now with the same modern conveniences and technologies and medicines and modes of travel and an information highway. We start with the last first to examine the differences which transpired during just one generation around 1888 until his departure in 1990. The differences will likely shock younger generations who grew up in the electronic age. The information age of course exploded with the development of the information highway called the internet. Information could be transmitted much faster and in much larger quantities over networks which eventually traveled most places on earth.

This was not the case in the early nineteen hundreds as the old familiar book shelves and libraries required a serious collection in order to have a well-rounded knowledge in multiple areas of study. The truth is old writings from scrolls to books had been a mode for the transfer of knowledge probably since the beginning of time dating from the record of Genesis which most bible scholars believe Moses to be the chosen writer of the creation record. It is also beneficial to note that Adam named all the creatures God created which when you think about required an incredible mind and memory in and of itself. So, the change from predominately books and manuscript which had been the most used up until this one generation and the onset of digital text technology began.

"Many shall run to and fro" is a phrase which seemingly refers to the increase in travel that will occur at the time of the end.

Transportation around just a hundred years ago looked a little different than the present. One example of the differences between transportation then and now is the fact that up until steam and combustible engines used in the 1800's the horse and buggy or chariot and horse had been one of the main means of mobility throughout generations, in areas that had horses anyway, along with choosing to walk or run in order to journey to a destination.

This slowly changed as the steam engine powered trains and boats and eventually the development of the first fully functioning automobile in the late nineteenth century. My granddad's traveling options in his younger years were horse and buggy. This changed in his older years as he drove one of the earliest model trucks. In overview, the main mode of travel in just one generation went from horses, one of the earliest forms of transportation to automobiles all the way to a space craft orbiting the earth between some hundred years of his lifetime. This makes the jewel of truth in the book of Daniel that "many shall run to and fro" at the time of the end extremely significant in the light of much of the technology in its initial development and progress had taken place in one generation.

One of my younger cousins may have had no idea some older vehicle windows had to be turned manually because all he had grown up with was electric windows. So, trying to explain to a younger generation how times were before electronics probably seems foreign to them and that was only around a fifteen-year difference. This is especially a different outlook when you consider some areas of the United States didn't have electrical capacity until the 1950's.

Many grandparents grew up without electricity or modern conveniences at a time when out houses were common instead of restrooms, and most were outside so rain or snow, cold or hot, light or dark, snakes or animals, a walk to the restroom was much different then. Old wood burning stoves and fireplaces were utilized for cooking or heating the house from the cold, and candle or oil lamp lights were used at night. Much of the food was home grown or sold in small local markets and entertainment probably involved a decent amount of time and money for travel and expenses. Clothes were washed using scrub boards with homemade soap and hung up on the old clothes lines to dry. Many families raised their own animals to eat and used salt curing or smoke houses to hang the meat and procure it as long as possible. These processes took time and energy and often involved the whole family pitching in to help. How wonderful a time this must have been with families working together, even though the people of that generation in the not-so-distant past had days full of challenges of their own.

Imagine the hard-working folks who trusted in Jesus and enjoyed old fashioned worship in the old church houses with fellowships and dinners on the ground filled with fun and laughter. A time when people joined together for barn raisings or using their trade skills to help build new homes or churches. Of course, it would not be right to forget the old family cemeteries behind old traditional churches where after fellowship dinners, people would walk through the rows of generations gone by of precious grandma's and grandpa's and aunts and uncles, along with distant family too far back to remember except for maybe a mention of a story of an aging granny reminiscing about those in the generation before them.

Now that we have examined in length some biblical facts which detail major historical events and time periods, we will examine the biblical viewpoints of God's Righteous and Holy Standards and how they endure forever. The Word of God teaches His Righteousness endureth forever and that He is the only wise Potentate. The scripture describes events in the New Testament book of Revelation and how the angels cry Holy, Holy, Holy. A closer look into the word holy is clean or pure. The opposite of holy may be considered unclean or defiled, or something that has been made unclean through contact with something corrupted that defiles something that may have been previously clean. God's standard of righteousness is part of His divine Holy nature. The Bible declares God is a Spirit and they that worship Him must worship Him in spirit and in truth. It also proclaims God is a consuming fire. For what the law could not do, in that it was weak through the flesh, God sending his own Son in the likeness of sinful flesh, and for sin, condemned sin in the flesh (Romans 8:3):

The law the scripture was referring to is the Law of God given by Moses written upon stone tablets. The scripture teaches there is none righteous, no not one. So, God's standard of righteousness was not attained through people even trying their best to keep the law because they were weak in their flesh. The spirit is willing but the flesh is weak. This is why some people try so hard to be righteous at times, only to make mistakes at other times. The Old Testament law required animal sacrifices for the sins of the people and designated priests (Levites) to carry out the office and duties of the temple and offer the sacrifices for the people.

Every year the high priest was commanded to offer up sacrifices which required the shedding of the blood of the animal's life. The principle concerning the cleansing of sin by the blood was required because the wages of sin is death, and that without the shedding of blood there is no remission of sin. Therefore, sin is a violation of God's standards and righteousness and is considered evil and wicked; iniquity and trespass are terms used to describe the variations of violations all known to be sin in the sight of the Almighty. Be not deceived God is not mocked for whatsoever a man soweth that shall he also reap.

The Holy Scripture concludes all under sin. David said something along the lines of being brought forth in iniquity from his mother's womb. Adam and Eve's fall to the serpent because they disobeyed God brought sin into the world and consequently gave satan the title of the god of this world. Sometimes people question the suffering of innocent little ones and some even seem to direct it toward a loving God. The truth is when evil infiltrated this world through sin it brought its devastating effects with it. The really sad part of the evil effects of sin is that it often affects the most innocent. For example, when adults make choices to abuse drugs or alcohol the young children are the ones who are often left hungry or neglected or beaten or worse or watch their mother's abuse.

This is why God hates sin because sin hurts the innocent little ones who God created, as well as those who harm themselves with self-destructive behavior. The scripture teaches we were made in His image and in His likeness, and we are the temple of God. The bible is really clear that if we defile the temple of God, God will destroy it for we are the temple of God. Therefore, people are held liable for the works they do in their own bodies. However, if children have been victims of abuse or neglect, then they should not feel guilty for the pain or abuse or neglect they suffered at the hand of someone who chose to do evil instead of good. Therefore, it is not a child's fault for what may have happened to them or even the pain and guilt that may haunt them, it is not their fault.

The current times display a very troubling trend along the timeline to the culmination and judgment of this wicked world. The scripture teaches if we are ashamed of the Lord Jesus in this evil and untoward generation, the Lord will be ashamed of us before His Father and the Holy Angels. In another place, the scripture teaches if we are ashamed of Him in this evil and adulterous generation, the Lord will be ashamed of us before His Father and the Holy Angels. This was written and told during generations long past where sin was not nearly abounding as it is today in our society and in our generation. Now the Old Testament is clear that there is nothing new under the sun, so sin and evil are often repeated by generations just in different forms or names, or even hidden beneath deceit to seemingly appear acceptable behavior.

The sins of past generations are explored in various stops throughout bible history. Some even became accepted practice and accepted among groups of people in various regions and displeased the Creator of heaven and earth who made every living creature. There were heathens whose wicked practices involved defiling themselves with mankind or other abominations in the eyes of the Most High. There was also idol worship throughout generations of old which worshiped objects they made of silver and gold and of wood and layered with gold, and called them their gods. This also displeased the true and living God which gave breath to man. For though there be that are called gods, whether in heaven or in earth, (as there be gods many, and lords many,) but to us there is but one God, the Father, of whom are all things, and we in him; and one Lord Jesus Christ, by whom are all things, and we by him (I Corinthians 8: 5, 6).

HE WHO IS TO COME

Who to Trust

The bible teaches God gave His chosen people the children of Israel the land He had promised to them. Moreover, He gave them commandments to observe concerning following the Lord to do right and good. He also gave them commandment not to serve other gods.

Deuteronomy 12:28-32

> *28.) Observe and hear all these words which I command thee, that it may go well with thee, and with thy children after thee forever, when thou doest that which is good and right in the sight of the LORD thy God.*

> *29.) When the LORD thy God shall cut off the nations from before thee, whither thou goest to possess them, and thou succeedest them, and dwellest in their land;*

> *30.) Take heed to thyself that thou be not snared by following them, after that they be destroyed from before thee; and that thou enquire not after their gods, saying, How did these nations serve their gods? even so will I do likewise.*

> *31.) Thou shalt not do so unto the LORD thy God: for every abomination to the LORD, which he hateth, have they done unto their gods; for even their sons and their daughters they have burnt in the fire to their gods.*

> *32.) What thing soever I command you, observe to do it: thou shalt not add thereto, nor diminish from it.*

However, even amongst God's holy nation after they inherited the land and had been warned against serving the false gods and or idols and not to commit the abominations of the heathen, some generations turned to doing just that. The bible teaches rebellion is as the sin of witchcraft, and in another place covetousness which is idolatry. We had not known lust unless the scripture had said though shalt not covet. There was a time Paul spoke of in the New Testament while preaching in Athens on Mars Hill that there was a time when God winked at such things, but now commandeth all men everywhere to repent.

Acts 17:22-34

> 22.) *Then Paul stood in the midst of Mars' hill, and said, Ye men of Athens, I perceive that in all things ye are too superstitious.*
>
> 23.) *For as I passed by, and beheld your devotions, I found an altar with this inscription, TO THE UNKNOWN GOD. Whom therefore ye ignorantly worship, him declare I unto you.*
>
> 24.) *God that made the world and all things therein, seeing that he is Lord of heaven and earth, dwelleth not in temples made with hands;*
>
> 25.) *Neither is worshipped with men's hands, as though he needed anything, seeing he giveth to all life, and breath, and all things;*
>
> 26.) *And hath made of one blood all nations of men for to dwell on all the face of the earth, and hath determined the times before appointed, and the bounds of their habitation;*
>
> 27.) *That they should seek the Lord, if haply they might feel after him, and find him, though he be not far from every one of us:*
>
> 28.) *For in him we live, and move, and have our being; as certain also of your own poets have said, For we are also his offspring.*
>
> 29.) *Forasmuch then as we are the offspring of God, we ought not to think that the Godhead is like unto gold, or silver, or stone, graven by art and man's device.*
>
> 30.) *And the times of this ignorance God winked at; but now commandeth all men every where to repent:*
>
> 31.) *Because he hath appointed a day, in the which he will judge the world in righteousness by that man whom he hath ordained; whereof he hath given assurance unto all men, in that he hath raised him from the dead.*
>
> 32.) *And when they heard of the resurrection of the dead, some mocked: and others said, We will hear thee again of this matter.*
>
> 33.) *So Paul departed from among them.*
>
> 34.) *Howbeit certain men clave unto him, and believed: among the which was Dionysius the Areopagite, and a woman named Damaris, and others with them.*

Evil men and seducers shall wax worse and worse deceiving and being deceived. The lust of this world hath blinded their minds so they won't believe. So if we had not known lust except the commandment had said thou shalt not covet, and covetousness is as the sin of idolatry, then let's examine the root of the matter. What is the root of the problem? What is at the core intention that caused the problem to sprout? What is the solution to the origin of the problem in order to stop the process from spreading further? What are the consequences of not finding the answers? Are the results reversible? How can I get help and or who will help me? Is it too late for me to get the help I need?

The answers to these deeper questions concerning the difference between the righteous standards of God and His divine Spiritual laws and principles that govern His creation and the rebellion of man to sin against God and those standards is an age-old question. The first question of what is the root of the problem requires us to examine the principle and then the testimonies of God which reveal His righteous judgments upon varying situations. The Lord loveth judgment and He is known by the judgment which he executeth, and mercy rejoiceth over judgment. So, if we are going to discover the root of sin we must understand what sin is and why people would choose to sin. However, even before we can explore the causes of sin we must examine God's character to discover what and why He calls evil and wickedness sin, and why sin to man must be seen as exceedingly sinful.

God is love and God is holy, and all power in heaven and earth the Bible teaches was given unto Jesus. God created all things so all things were created by Him and for Him, even the wicked for the day of destruction. His ways are higher than our ways and His judgments past finding out. God the Father of our Lord Jesus Christ is great and greatly to be praised and greatly to be feared. This is why the scripture stresses do we persuade God or man. Do we attempt to even think to persuade God a holy and loving God to accept vile wickedness which is against His divine nature and His laws? Forsake not your own mercy and be wise to seek and do good. We should seek to persuade man and warn man to deliver themselves from this present evil world, to repent of their evil ways and their sin before they are destroyed.

So, an exploration of the truth in scripture concerning the past involves God creating and placing man in the Garden of Eden. Of course, God is eternal and the garden was where the tree of life was so man had access to the tree of life. However, the most subtle creature of the garden was lurking to attack man whom God had made in His image; male and female created them. This may be why the scripture teaches we wrestle not against flesh and blood but against principalities and powers, spiritual wickedness in high places. So, we must find where this spiritual wickedness in high places is, and who is a possible source and who is in league with this evil force.

Isaiah 14:12-17

12.) How art thou fallen from heaven, O Lucifer, son of the morning! how art thou cut down to the ground, which didst weaken the nations!

13.) For thou hast said in thine heart, I will ascend into heaven, I will exalt my throne above the stars of God: I will sit also upon the mount of the congregation, in the sides of the north:

14.) I will ascend above the heights of the clouds; I will be like the most High.

15.) Yet thou shalt be brought down to hell, to the sides of the pit.

16.) They that see thee shall narrowly look upon thee, and consider thee, saying, is this the man that made the earth to tremble, that did shake kingdoms;

17.) That made the world as a wilderness, and destroyed the cities thereof; that opened not the house of his prisoners?

It is amazing how God spoke and embedded messages within messages to the holy prophets even as he was revealing maybe a present issue of the time and the details concerning an event or situation and suddenly a burst of revelation concerning eternal dynamics and future times, generations, and people, or reveals a mystery about a spiritual adversary or adversaries. Thus, Satan which means adversary was being exposed as Lucifer, and the terrible spiritual heart condition which led him to think he could exalt his throne (authority, power) above the stars of God. Thus, the connection is made between spiritual wickedness in high places and the principalities and powers they seek to impose.

Nevertheless, God is the Alpha and Omega, the beginning and the end, the first and the last, and the heavens of heavens could not contain Him as He has to humble Himself even to behold the earth. Yet He has respect to the lowly, and is nigh them who are of a broken and contrite spirit as blessed are the poor in spirit. So, God set the times in order and the history search of the Holy Text brings His Master plan into plain sight throughout times past. The genealogy of Jesus and His miraculous birth of virgin with child, and the genealogical record provided in the New Testament displays God's marvelous design to bring forth the savior into the world at the appointed time to destroy the works of the devil, and save souls from their sins.

Furthermore, since the Lord assuredly prepared the times past, and those times have merged to bring forth the savior and the gospel of Jesus Christ to be preached throughout all the world. The faith of Jesus Christ has impacted more people than any other since His birth in the flesh to now in our present generation since the times of our Savior in the flesh in

Israel a couple of thousand years ago to the evangelization of nearly all kindreds and tongues. The scripture teaches when the gospel has been preached throughout to all nations; the end would be sure. So, most certainly, since the past and present have the blueprint so to speak of the Almighty, so the future and the last day will certainly as well, just as He has outlined in His holy Word the times of the end.

Matthew 24:1-51

1.) *And Jesus went out, and departed from the temple: and his disciples came to him for to shew him the buildings of the temple.*

2.) *And Jesus said unto them, See ye not all these things? verily I say unto you, There shall not be left here one stone upon another, that shall not be thrown down.*

3.) *And as he sat upon the mount of Olives, the disciples came unto him privately, saying, Tell us, when shall these things be? and what shall be the sign of thy coming, and of the end of the world?*

4.) *And Jesus answered and said unto them, Take heed that no man deceive you.*

5.) *For many shall come in my name, saying, I am Christ; and shall deceive many.*

6.) *And ye shall hear of wars and rumours of wars: see that ye be not troubled: for all these things must come to pass, but the end is not yet.*

7.) *For nation shall rise against nation, and kingdom against kingdom: and there shall be famines, and pestilences, and earthquakes, in divers places.*

8.) *All these are the beginning of sorrows.*

9.) *Then shall they deliver you up to be afflicted, and shall kill you: and ye shall be hated of all nations for my name's sake.*

10.) *And then shall many be offended, and shall betray one another, and shall hate one another.*

11.) *And many false prophets shall rise, and shall deceive many.*

12.) *And because iniquity shall abound, the love of many shall wax cold.*

13.) *But he that shall endure unto the end, the same shall be saved.*

14.) *And this gospel of the kingdom shall be preached in all the world for a witness unto all nations; and then shall the end come.*

15.) *When ye therefore shall see the abomination of desolation, spoken of by Daniel the prophet, stand in the holy place, (whoso readeth, let him understand:)*

16.) *Then let them which be in Judaea flee into the mountains:*

17.) *Let him which is on the housetop not come down to take any thing out of his house:*

18.) *Neither let him which is in the field return back to take his clothes.*

19.) *And woe unto them that are with child, and to them that give suck in those days!*

20.) *But pray ye that your flight be not in the winter, neither on the sabbath day:*

21.) *For then shall be great tribulation, such as was not since the beginning of the world to this time, no, nor ever shall be.*

22.) *And except those days should be shortened, there should no flesh be saved: but for the elect's sake those days shall be shortened.*

23.) *Then if any man shall say unto you, Lo, here is Christ, or there; believe it not.*

24.) *For there shall arise false Christs, and false prophets, and shall shew great signs and wonders; insomuch that, if it were possible, they shall deceive the very elect.*

25.) *Behold, I have told you before.*

26.) *Wherefore if they shall say unto you, Behold, he is in the desert; go not forth: behold, he is in the secret chambers; believe it not.*

27.) *For as the lightning cometh out of the east, and shineth even unto the west; so shall also the coming of the Son of man be.*

28.) *For wheresoever the carcase is, there will the eagles be gathered together.*

29.) *Immediately after the tribulation of those days shall the sun be darkened, and the moon shall not give her light, and the stars shall fall from heaven, and the powers of the heavens shall be shaken:*

30.) *And then shall appear the sign of the Son of man in heaven: and then shall all the tribes of the earth mourn, and they shall see the Son of man coming in the clouds of heaven with power and great glory.*

31.) *And he shall send his angels with a great sound of a trumpet, and they shall gather together his elect from the four winds, from one end of heaven to the other.*

32.) *Now learn a parable of the fig tree; When his branch is yet tender, and putteth forth leaves, ye know that summer is nigh:*

33.) *So likewise ye, when ye shall see all these things, know that it is near, even at the doors.*

34.) *Verily I say unto you, This generation shall not pass, till all these things be fulfilled.*

35.) *Heaven and earth shall pass away, but my words shall not pass away.*

36.) *But of that day and hour knoweth no man, no, not the angels of heaven, but my Father only.*

37,) *But as the days of Noe were, so shall also the coming of the Son of man be.*

38.) For as in the days that were before the flood they were eating and drinking, marrying and giving in marriage, until the day that Noe entered into the ark,

39.) And knew not until the flood came, and took them all away; so shall also the coming of the Son of man be.

40.) Then shall two be in the field; the one shall be taken, and the other left.

41.) Two women shall be grinding at the mill; the one shall be taken, and the other left.

42.) Watch therefore: for ye know not what hour your Lord doth come.

43.) But know this, that if the goodman of the house had known in what watch the thief would come, he would have watched, and would not have suffered his house to be broken up.

44.) Therefore be ye also ready: for in such an hour as ye think not the Son of man cometh.

45.) Who then is a faithful and wise servant, whom his lord hath made ruler over his household, to give them meat in due season?

46.) Blessed is that servant, whom his lord when he cometh shall find so doing.

47.) Verily I say unto you, That he shall make him ruler over all his goods.

48.) But and if that evil servant shall say in his heart, My lord delayeth his coming;

49.) And shall begin to smite his fellowservants, and to eat and drink with the drunken;

50.) The lord of that servant shall come in a day when he looketh not for him, and in an hour that he is not aware of,

51.) And shall cut him asunder, and appoint him his portion with the hypocrites: there shall be weeping and gnashing of teeth.

Verse fourteen states: and this gospel of the kingdom shall be preached in all the world for a witness unto all nations; and then shall the end come. The truth is all the way back to the fifteen hundreds the gospel of Christ had made tremendous progress reaching throughout Europe. Many Missionaries have also prayed and ventured to the continent of Africa in order to preach the gospel of Jesus Christ, the saving power of God through His Son. Paul the apostle was initially led by the Holy Spirit not to go into Asia at that certain time, but later took the gospel into Asia at the appointed time. The apostle John also wrote of the Churches in Asia in the New Testament book of Revelation.

The gospel has also visited extensively the regions of North and South America, as the gospel was a founding factor for early settlers from Europe into North America. The gospel has since been propelled throughout vast regions of the globe as a result of the evangelism of the Church in America and specifically the Jesus film. Many tribes and languages of indigenous people have had the bible translated into their language, and estimates have put the translations of bibles into every language of every tribe and people in range to possibly fulfill the words of Christ Jesus in the not-so-distant future, "and this gospel of the kingdom shall be preached in all the world for a witness unto all nations; and then shall the end come."

In Summary, we have discussed a source of sin and deception which is the enemy of every man's soul, Satan. His heart was lifted up with pride against the Almighty God and his punishment was being cast down to hell. However, a closer look at spiritual occasions in scripture where the devil and his purposes are described will help us understand the realm and strategies of the deceiver. Many bible scholars believe Lucifer was a created being and point to the Old Testament book of Ezekiel as evidence. Ezekiel describes him as the anointed cherub that covereth and explains his immense beauty which seemed to be a focus in his pride and corruption. He was also described as having musical instruments built into him seemingly for worshiping the true and living God. His place was also amongst the stones of fire in the holy mountain.

Ezekiel 28:13-17

> *13.) Thou hast been in Eden the garden of God; every precious stone was thy covering, the sardius, topaz, and the diamond, the beryl, the onyx, and the jasper, the sapphire, the emerald, and the carbuncle, and gold: the workmanship of thy tabrets and of thy pipes was prepared in thee in the day that thou wast created.*
>
> *14.) Thou art the anointed cherub that covereth; and I have set thee so: thou wast upon the holy mountain of God; thou hast walked up and down in the midst of the stones of fire.*
>
> *15.) Thou wast perfect in thy ways from the day that thou wast created, till iniquity was found in thee.*
>
> *16.) By the multitude of thy merchandise they have filled the midst of thee with violence, and thou hast sinned: therefore I will cast thee as profane out*
>
> *of the mountain of God: and I will destroy thee, O covering cherub, from the midst of the stones of fire.*
>
> *17.) Thine heart was lifted up because of thy beauty, thou hast corrupted thy wisdom by reason of thy brightness: I will cast thee to the ground, I will lay thee before kings, that they may behold thee.*

The testimonies of God are given through the guidance of the recorded texts of events of people and their true stories and histories accounted for by just how the Lord dealt with certain situations in specific or under general circumstances. The testimonies of God are of major importance because understanding the will of God allows a person to discern right and wrong in a specific instance and in a specific time when that may be challenging when some maybe through ignorance or deception are saying the contrary. For example, Jesus healed a man on one occasion and told him to go and sin no more less a worse thing come upon you. On another occasion, Jesus would tell people their faith had made them whole. Furthermore, Jesus yet again was asked whether the man or his parents had sinned when talking about a man who was born blind. Jesus' response was that neither the man nor his parents had sinned, but it was for the glory of God, and Jesus healed the man who was born blind.

The scripture also talks about a spirit of infirmity, maybe like fear that's not from God for the fear of God brings strong confidence. The scripture is also clear that we were not given the spirit of fear but of power and of love and of a sound mind. So, fear, worry, stress, and fretting can cause major health problems as has been commonly well known and studied. Joy, peace, and love on the other hand help people to enjoy the blessings of God He has so graciously and mercifully provided for people whether they are doing evil or good a lot of times. The Bible teaches He causes it to rain on the just and the unjust and that we should be perfect as our Father which is in heaven is perfect and shew mercy. What was pleasing unto the Lord about the actions of His creation, or what displeased God about the actions of His creation?

Why wouldn't God withhold rain from people who were doing evil? He has in certain times allowed drought and withheld rain, but why not until all evil is wiped out? His mercy endureth forever, and the scripture teaches He doesn't take pleasure in the destruction of the wicked. Mercy and the knowledge of the Holy One may reach to the heart of generations and change them by turning them to His truth to do good. Some may do good and some may do evil but God gives people time to repent. The scripture also discusses the day of visitation of God to deal with a person and give them a chance to choose Him. Also, many righteous could live in an area and hate the evil around them, thus a war between the good and evil like today in capitol buildings within legislatures some fighting for good and some evil and when the balance is off people are oppressed and iniquity may be framed in a law or laws. Nevertheless, God is not slack concerning slackness but is longsuffering toward us not willing that any should perish but that all should come to the knowledge of the truth.

Job was a perfect and upright man according to God's evaluation of Job's good works on earth and his intercession for his family. The Bible reveals on a certain day when the sons of God came to stand before God that satan also came before God. God basically asked satan where he had been, and he told God he had been going to and fro in the earth. Similarly, the scripture details that satan as a roaring lion goeth about seeking whom he may devour. God asked the adversary if he had considered his servant Job. The enemy responded to the effect that God had placed a hedge of protection about him and if it were removed, he would curse God to his face. God then allowed him to touch Job but not take his life. In one day, Job's servants came in one by one to tell Job evil tidings involving the loss of his children and his possessions. Job's response in his horrible situation was that he mourned and still blessed God in all his pain.

The enemy came before God again and the conversation was how Job did not curse God despite the enemy's attacks. The next move the enemy made was to say skin for skin and to suggest Job would curse God if it were his own life on the line. So, satan was allowed to touch Job's flesh with boils sore and grievous boil from his head to his feet. Job scraped his sores with a potsherd and sat in ashes and mourned. Job's wife told him he should curse God and die, but Job said you speak as a foolish woman shall we receive good at the hand of God and not receive evil. So, Job in his increasing suffering and pain cursed his day but did not curse God. His friends came to comfort him and when they saw him afar off they didn't recognize him and wept.

His friends sat with him in silence for a good while seemingly in silence and then Job began to speak of his great sorrow and struggle. His friends increasingly began to accuse Job of sin or wickedness after they heard him maintain his innocence and integrity. The verbal assaults became so intense at one point that Job told them your wisdom perish with you. God after much discourse between Job and his friends' accusations revealed Himself to Job out of the whirlwind and asked Job specific questions to show Job His power in creation and His infinite knowledge and understanding. Job repented because he had heard of the Almighty by the hearing of the ear but now had seen the power of the Almighty. God also rebuked Job's friends and told them Job had spoken the right thing concerning Him and they were commanded to go to Job. God turned the captivity of Job when he prayed for his friends and God blessed Job with twice as much as he had before.

The scripture teaches in the Old Testament that the world has been set in men's hearts. The scripture also teaches we should pray for wisdom from God because like the truth of God's Word in Job not every situation or circumstance of man is the same. For instance, the bible teaches man looks at the outward appearance, but God looks at the heart. We are also not to judge anything before its time. So, we see clearly by examining the account and testimony of Job that things are not always as they appear. Sometimes people may seem afflicted like they must have done evil to deserve such afflictions, but the case concerning Job was the opposite. A similar perspective in the New Testament book of James warns against showing partiality because of a person's wealth or poverty in the church.

Ecclesiastes 3: 11: He hath made everything beautiful in his time: also he hath set the world in their heart, so that no man can find out the work that God maketh from the beginning to the end.

The New Testament of the Holy Bible is clear that without faith it is impossible to please God, because we must believe that He is and that He is a rewarder of them that diligently seek Him. Jesus secures this good faith principle when He heard the message of the centurion who sent to Jesus for to heal his servant whom he loved. The centurion asked the Lord basically to speak the word only and his servant would be healed. He explained he also was a man under authority (or in power) and he would tell his servants what to do and they would do it. Jesus said he had not seen such great faith no not in Israel. This is amazing how a man who had only heard of Jesus but didn't feel worthy to even go to Him or for Jesus to even enter into his house (humility) understood that Jesus had power over the natural and spiritual realms to just say it because He has power to command it to be and it is.

Now the second principle regarding obedience to our Creator is the principle of humility. Proverbs 29:23; a man's pride shall bring him low: but honour shall uphold the humble in spirit. Jesus also confirmed this principle in his obedience of being found in fashion as a man He humbled himself and became obedient unto death wherefore God hath also highly exalted Him and given Him a name which is above every name that at the name of Jesus every knee shall bow and tongue confess that Jesus Christ is Lord. So, the Old and New Testaments consistently verify the principle of man's need to humble themselves under the hand of Almighty God. Therefore, the earlier proposed question of how can we get help is answered by the principle of humility and the fear of the Lord.

How does the enemy of our souls work to try and destroy God's children and why does the devil hate God's children so much. The answers to these questions begins with why does he hate God. The answer is envy.

The enemy wanted to be like God in an evil sense to seemingly try and cast God down from His Excellency. The problem satan had is the same many have today who rebel against God and His laws. There is no wisdom against God. God understands and knows the heart of man and the thoughts before man can even think them because His greatness is unsearchable and His judgments past finding out. So, submission to the God of all creation is good, while stubbornness or resisting God's will can bring lots of trouble and anguish.

Man was made in God's image therefore satan hates man. Man is God's workmanship therefore the devil hates man. Man can worship and glorify God which the old serpent hates. Thus, two kingdoms and principalities are at work in the world. God's kingdom is the kingdom of Truth, Jesus is the way the Truth and the life and no man comes to the Father but by Him whose scepter is righteousness, and the kingdom of darkness which enemy is built of lies for the devil is a liar and the father of lies and a murderer from the beginning and is an evil kingdom.

John makes real plain when he wrote about the matter in the holy text as he that doeth good is of God, and he that doeth sin is of the devil. Jesus also once again verifies this when he told some leaders of His day that they were of their father the devil and the works of their father they will do. Of course, satan had been around long before that generation to be called their father, as he was the wicked one who influenced Cain to kill Abel his brother in the book of Genesis in the beginning of times.

So a key concept to understanding the web of influence and order of operations throughout the ages is to understand that the enemy still uses the same evil influences today as he has used in the past to go about as a roaring lion seeking whom he may devour. This is why a God-fearing person when he sees evil coming discerns the evil and hides himself in the secret place of the most high and seeks guidance for deliverance from evil in the protective arms of the Lord. However, an evil doer may ignore the warning signs and be punished. This is why we can pray God have mercy and send laborers into the harvest so souls can be saved, or even for forgiveness for a saint who has sinned a sin not unto death.

Therefore, the answer to the earlier question of whether or not sin is irreversible is sort of yes and no. Not necessarily irreversible, once a sin has occurred there must be a payment for that sin in order to reconcile a soul to righteousness with a Holy God. However, there can be remission of sin which the bible teaches without the shedding of blood there is no remission of sin. The best time to avoid sin is before sin occurs in a number of possible states. For instance, the closer a soul gets to the actual point of sin usually several things have occurred before hand. Close to the line of sin generally involves the yielding unto a potential or imminent temptation. The bible is clear that God cannot be tempted with evil neither tempteth He any man but every man is tempted when he is drawn away of his own lust and enticed. There is no temptation that is not common to man, but with the temptation will also make a way of escape that he may be able to bear it. He knows how to deliver the Godly out of temptation.

These states of temptation can be knowingly or ignorantly either way depending upon the type of sin or the state of the person being tempted. This is likely one reason the bible warns "not to give place to the devil" because in doing so a person would be easy prey for the tempter to trap. The other deals with "My people perish for lack of knowledge" which deals with possibly presumptuous sins. Now if a person does not have the knowledge of the truth because they have not heard the truth of the good news of the gospel, then they are much more likely to sin out of ignorance that their actions are even sinful. The Old Testament teaches that once a person realized they had broken a law or commandment of God then they were at that time that they were completely conscience of their trespass to take a sacrifice offering for that sin.

The New Testament teaches unbelievers should repent and believe in Jesus Christ that He is the Son of God who came to take away the sin of the world. The scripture actually details the fact that He became sin for us. He became the sacrifice for sin by the shedding of His own holy blood which was completely sinless. He was tempted in every measure as a man yet without sin. So, we could not pay for our own or anyone else sin because all have sinned and fall short of the glory of God, only Jesus could pay the ultimate price for our sins.

So, to further clarify the answer to whether or not sin is irreversible the truth is Jesus paid the ransom for our sin and actually became a curse for us; as the scripture teaches cursed is anyone who hangs on a tree. The curse of sin and its effects of death were taken upon Jesus at the cross; therefore, like Jesus explained whosoever believeth in me shall never die. They didn't understand Jesus was offering them everlasting life for He died for the sins of the whole world. The mercy of God extends to everyone because it's His to give along with His grace for He was and is full of grace and truth. He leadeth me in the paths of righteousness for His name's sake. He restoreth my soul.

Jesus has the keys of death, hell, and the grave and all power in heaven and in earth was given unto Him after His resurrection from the dead. The devil is still on the hunt for souls as he is referred to as the accuser of the brethren in the New Testament book of revelation. The scripture unveils that day and night the enemy accuses the brethren, but the scripture also teaches we have an advocate with the Father, Jesus Christ the Righteous. The scripture also gives the formula for overcoming the accusations of Satan. They overcame him by the blood of the lamb and the word of their testimony. So, the power of forgiveness of sins through the holy blood of Jesus and the word of our testimony allow believers to overcome the enemy. If any man be in Christ, he is a new creature, old things have passed away behold all things have become new. Thus, the famous phrase Jesus told Nicodemus that except a man be born again he cannot enter into the kingdom of God, for he must be born again not of flesh and blood but of water and of the Spirit.

This leads us to the question of how does a believer live a victorious life once he is born again through or by faith in Jesus Christ. The bible teaches the calling of God is not by the will of man, nor by the will of the flesh, but by the will of God. Therefore, a man must have the eyes of his understanding enlightened with the knowledge of the truth and that is from the Lord. For no man can come unto the Lord except the Father draw him. So, there are two diametrically opposed forces at work like we discussed earlier but on a very personal level. The two forces are the divine nature of God, the Spirit of God which he offers to those who obey Him, and the corruptible fleshly nature which can defile the souls of men if not brought under subjection by the Spirit.

A real interesting verse from the treasures of wisdom and understanding in the light of the truth reveals just how powerful the controlling of one's spirit really is. The Old Testament text goes something like this; a man who hath not power over his own spirit is like a city without walls. Maybe we should back up a little to clarify the way God created man and the essential parts of His masterpiece. God made man from the dust and God breathed into man and man became a living soul. So, the flesh part of man was derived from the dust and of course we know the flesh will return to the dust after death and corruption of the flesh or until the day of redemption of the purchased possession, which is sealed by the Holy Spirit of promise, the resurrection for those whose souls are saved.

Part two of the discussion is; God breathed into man's nostrils and man became a living soul. So, life did not enter into man just by being made flesh and blood from the dust form. The New Testament also clarifies this in James where it confirms; the body without the spirit is dead. Of course, this is evident to anyone who has ever been to a funeral where a body was viewed. The body is lifeless though fully intact because the spirit of the person has left their body and then the body begins the process of corruption like it has since creation. Currently, world population data places the birthrate above the death rate thus an increasing overall population. So, a closer comparison of the natural and spiritual births and the impact of each may help us realize which is more important.

David's prayer is recorded in Psalms which may help us better prioritize our lives. He prayed that the Lord may teach us to number our days that we might apply our hearts unto wisdom. The bible thousands of years ago revealed how man's years would be three score and ten and if by reason of strength four score. Therefore, looking at recent data the average age is exactly between those ages just like it was written. Therefore, if we take a close look at our lives and number our days we begin to see just as the scripture explains life is like a vapor. It is so true that it seems like time goes by so quickly when remembering old times from ones youth or childhood. We ourselves and others as the aging process take its course even on the healthiest of individuals and the truth is told plainly in God's holy book when it teaches concerning death that there is no discharge in that war, and that no man can keep alive his own soul.

A soul that just walks after the desires of their own fleshly nature will likely not even know they are being controlled by their evil fleshly desires. Now please do not misunderstand the difference between the good senses God gave us to taste, smell, touch, see, and hear. The good Lord gave us all things richly to enjoy and children learn through all these channels because we were fearfully and wonderfully made. So, God chose to allow growth and development at the perfect rate and speed by His divine design. This is why if the body begins to grow too quickly or too slowly, the body can have health issues. Once and again, we see a wonderful parallel between the natural body and the spiritual body about balance, goodness, and righteousness. For example, the bible teaches that believers should exhibit moderation in their lives to do good and live by the righteous example of Jesus Christ the Lord.

The difference between the flesh and spirit the scripture refers to is talking about every persons struggle to either follow the good desires (love) opted to them or the evil desires (lust) opted to them. Remember, God made man upright but they sought out many inventions. Therefore, Christians have the similar responsibility God gave His chosen people the children of Israel to teach their children the testimonies of God like training them up in the way they should go and when they are old they will not depart from it. Jesus is the way the truth and the life so when children are taught in the good way of the Lord they are taught to show love and compassion in righteousness. Once again do not be deceived by the tempters snare of calling lust love to try and make any desire a good desire. The bible teaches God is love. The bible also teaches God hates evil.

Therefore, love cannot and never will include lust because God's Word is forever settled in the heavens. If I may speak boldly, God is not going to change His holy righteous word for you, me, or anybody else. He has never once altered His righteousness for He is the same yesterday today and forever and He changeth not. Therefore, He did not change His word when the children of Israel came out of Egyptian bondage by a strong hand

and destroyed the nations before them in the promise land. He also did not change His word when He gave Israel commandment that He would have no god before Him. He also executed His word to the prophets concerning evil kings who made wicked laws and desecrated the Holy Temple of God built by Solomon.

He also blessed kings who obeyed His word and returned to the Lord by obeying His commandments and tearing down the idols and abominations in the land, like when they destroyed the house of the Sodomites near the temple of God. He did not change His word when His own holy people turned to worship the false idol god the queen of heaven, but led them into captivity and destroyed the evil workers in strong judgment to cleanse the land. He also did not change His word when He spoke through Daniel of His mercy to save a remnant of His holy ones and restore them to their homeland after seventy years had been accomplished. He touched the hearts of the kings of the Medes and Persian like Cyrus who gave Ezra permission to rebuild Jerusalem with the help of the kings own treasury to fulfill His word.

He also did not change His word when Jesus Himself, the son of God in the flesh, prayed in the garden that this cup would pass from Him. The cup of suffering which Jesus would soon endure after He prayed nevertheless not my will but thine be done. What love of the Father who saw that Jesus His only begotten son would bring many to righteousness? God once more did not change His word when Jesus arose the third day and did not see corruption. God also did not change when He told Peter upon this rock I will build my church and the gates of hell will not prevail against it. After Peters many ups and downs during his discipleship from the Master, Peter preached on the day of Pentecost and thousands were saved. God did not change His word when Jesus told the disciples greater works ye shall do because I go to my Father and your Father.

The apostles thenceforth healed many of their infirmities and many notable miracles were done by them before the people, so much so, that the high priest and Pharisees who opposed them were well aware and afraid to punish them at times because the people might stone those leaders who were persecuting Jesus' disciple. God also did not change His word about the saving both Jews and Gentiles by His mercy as they received the Holy Ghost in the book of Acts just as the apostles had previously on the day of Pentecost. So, God's character has been revealed over the ages through His righteous judgments and mercy. God also did not change His word when He revealed Himself unto Saul in the New Testament. Saul was a Pharisee who consented when the great disciple Stephen was martyred and had received letters from the authorities to persecute Christians through death or imprisonment.

Saul was on his way to Damascus when a light from heaven shown around him and him and his entourage fell to the ground. He heard a voice asking him why he was persecuting Him, and that it was hard for him to kick against the pricks. Saul asked Him, who are you. He said I am Jesus whom you persecute. The group with him saw the light but didn't hear the voice. Saul was blinded and given direction to go for prayer to Ananias who God revealed to pray for Saul and when he did the scales fell from his eyes and he could see. Saul turned to Paul was also baptized and proceeded to serve the Lord Jesus with great fervor.

The Lord had revealed to Paul early on that he would suffer many things for the Lord's name. Paul was filled with the Spirit of God and began to spread the gospel throughout the Middle East and Asia after his revelation and conversion. Paul before his conversion was so zealous for the Law of Moses and the righteousness which is by the law of which he was blameless. However, he considered his own righteousness loss that he might win Christ and the hope of the resurrection. He initially missed God's righteousness by attempting to trust in his own righteousness. The scripture teaches that Jesus is the end of the law for righteousness. It also teaches Jesus did not come to destroy the law but to fulfill it.

God also did not change His word and faithfulness as some apostles preached in Antioch and they were first called Christians at Antioch. The bible is also very clear in the New Testament book of Acts that "God working with them" many miracles were done by the apostles. Furthermore, God's faithfulness shined through the midst of darkness when Paul and Silas had been persecuted, beaten, and imprisoned as they began to sing praise to God at midnight. The bible records an earthquake which opened the jail doors and caused the prison guard to try and take his own life because he thought the prisoners had escaped. He asked the question to the Paul and Silas "what must I do to be saved." They told him about Jesus and salvation and him and his whole house believed and was baptized.

Scripture reveals through Paul's writing how Paul suffered many things for the elects' sake. Wow, imagine the insight to understand that believers may face many perils to preach the gospel to those who will believe and be born again because God elected them to hear and believe. In another place the scripture teaches as many as thou hast called, and many are called but few chosen. The book of Acts provides details to the amazing grace and sovereignty in election for His love for people in sending His messengers to great lengths, even life and death circumstances of natural disasters, to reach with His message those who haven't had a chance to hear or due to their circumstances or where they live in remote regions.

The historic event took place on Paul's Journey to Rome after he appealed to Caesar when accused of the Jews and refusal to be turned over to their jurisdiction. Paul was being escorted by a Roman centurion and set sail in the Mediterranean in route to eventually make it to Rome. The weather seemed good at a place called fair havens even though the time for sailing was considered dangerous. Paul warned about the sailing venture to no avail after the captain of the ship saw the weather was good. Little did they know the good weather would be short lived and very temporary as the weather would soon deteriorate once having committed to the journey upon the sea. They soon sailed into possibly a cyclone like storm called Euroclydon which was so severe they were driven by the fierce winds. They cast out the tackle of the ship and let the wind drive the ship for many days without seeing light. So hungry and exhausted the men had given up all hope of being saved.

Amazing how sometimes we make decisions because the weather seems fair in our lives, but should have prayed for direction from the Almighty who sees the storm well before we do. The amazing part of this historic event is when all hope seemed loss the purpose of God was revealed to Paul. Paul told the crew they should take meat because they had not eaten for many days. He also told them they should have listened to him not to set sail and avoided the peril basically. He also informed them the angel of the Lord revealed to him the night before that no man's life would be lost but the ship would be lost. He also told them they must be cast upon a certain island and this revelation reveals the incredible miracle God was in the process of orchestrating.

Let us reason this through of how their ship was being driven by the wind in a fierce storm with absolutely no guidance of their own in the middle of the sea. Their lives had been in danger and the circumstances where completely out of their control. God's love is so wonderfully all-encompassing to seek and save that which is lost that He saw those precious souls on a remote island. The people were like barbarians with probably little contact with the regions outside of their isolated existence, but God sent a chosen vessel to pray for them and God healed them of sicknesses and likely preached to them the good news of Jesus Christ. Oh, the breadth and depth of the love of God which passeth knowledge.

The message Paul received came to pass just as it was told. The ship was destroyed, and they floated on pieces of the ship and made it to shore. The island people received them in the cold weather and Paul was picking up sticks for a fire and a serpent bit him. Originally, the islanders thought Paul had escaped the judgment of the sea but not the judgment of death from the serpent's bite. However, their knowledge of the beast being venomous they waited for Paul to swell up and die. Nevertheless, while they waited their minds soon changed when neither occurred and they thought Paul was a god. The miracle working hand of God was upon the life of Paul who God had sent to this particular island for His divine purpose and plan.

Romans 8: 20: For the creature was made subject to vanity, not willingly, but by reason of Him who hath subjected the same in hope. The wonderful hope from the Lord of the resurrection, eternal life, and the promise of a spiritual body are anchors to the soul, precious promises. The scripture teaches that believers have hope and should not sorrow as others who have no real hope without Christ the Savior. This hope in Jesus and through the love of Jesus causes our spirits to groan within us for the manifestation of the sons of God. This hope also is the hope promised in God's Holy Word of Truth (let God's Word be true and every man a liar) for man will return to the dust and the Lord is the light of our salvation of whom shall we be afraid, is the hope that this mortal must put on immortality. Jesus taught that if we believe in Him we will never die.

Therefore, man must choose who they are going to serve, the lust of the flesh or are they going to walk after the Spirit. The flesh lusteth against the spirit and the spirit against the flesh so that ye cannot do the things that ye would. For when we were in the flesh, the motions of sins, which were by the law, did work in our members to bring forth fruit unto death (Romans 7:5). I John 2 teaches the lust of the eyes, the lust of the flesh, and the pride of life are not of the Father, but of the world. These same temptations which were used on Eve led to Adam's fall. These temptations were also used on Jesus Christ Himself, however with no avail because He stood upon the Words of God, the Holy Scriptures, and the Truth and walked after His Fathers' will, after the Spirit. So, sin entered with the disobedience to God's commandment by Adam which led to death. This was explained to them before they ate of the tree of knowledge of good and evil and their decision even though tempted was still their decision which decision in turn caused sin and death upon those after them until the Savior King Jesus appeared in the flesh to save the world. The spiritual laws that govern the earth and man for all things were made by Him and for Him are revealed through the commandments and directives in the Holy Scriptures so we can trust and walk humbly with Him in faithfulness.

The Lord also made a decision to come to the earth "lo I come in the volume of the book it is written of Me. Sacrifice and burnt offering thou wouldst not but a body hast thou prepared Me. The savior of the world, creator, master, the Christ, the anointed one, the Son of the Living God has been prepared and given as a sacrifice for our sins, and not only for believers, but for the entire world. The greatness of God is unsearchable and His understanding infinite. This is why you can see early in the Old Testament signs of God's plan to send a savior to redeem man from their iniquities. This is an incredible mystery revealed from the early prophets declaring His day and times all the way to later prophets detailing the suffering Jesus would endure in His body to save men's souls. The word teaches by the understanding of His righteous servant, He shall justify many.

Furthermore, later prophets even detailed the times of the end and the glorious return of Jesus Christ the Son of God. The prophet Daniel stated something like the saints will possess the kingdom in the end. Therefore, the kingdom of God and of His son Jesus Christ shall have the dominion upon the earth. The meek shall inherit the earth the Lord taught in the New Testament book of Matthew which provides a great light in dark times of evil generations that the darkness will be overcome by the light. The true light appeared when Jesus was born to His precious mother Mary, the miraculous birth of the Savior of the world.

He came unto His own and His own received Him not. Jesus Christ the Lord actually gave a parable of how a husbandman left his vineyard to His servants to dress and tend when He went into a far country. So, afterward He sent servants to check the vineyard and they were evil entreated. So, lastly He sent His own son thinking surely they will honour the son. Nevertheless, the wicked servants saw the son coming and said let's kill him and the inheritance will be ours. What do you think the Lord will do to those wicked servants when He returns? Jesus taught the people this parable and then it happened just as he had explained. The good news is He also rose from the dead as He had told them He would, and He also explained how he would return. There is forgiveness with the Lord that He may be feared.

So, God is good and God is eternal and God is the Creator and God is righteous in all His ways and holy in all His works and His righteousness endureth forever and there is no unrighteousness in Him. Neither can He be tempted with evil. Let no man say when he is tempted, I am tempted of God: for God cannot be tempted with evil, neither tempteth he any man (James 1:13): But every man is tempted, when he is drawn away of his own lust, and enticed (James 1:14). Then when lust hath conceived, it bringeth forth sin: and sin, when it is finished, bringeth forth death (James 1:15). Therefore, God's standard is a standard of truth and righteous and by mercy and truth iniquity is purged. God created the naturals laws and His kingdom ruleth over all and His dominion is an eternal dominion, and His kingdom is an everlasting kingdom.

This is why truth will win over lies, falsehoods, false religions, false prophets and over all principalities and power for Jesus is the way, the truth, and the life and no man can come to the Father but by Jesus. There is no other name under heaven by which man must be saved. The scripture teaches those who believe in Jesus shall not perish but have everlasting life. In addition, the bible teaches whosoever will, let him come. Therefore, Jesus doesn't force a person against their own will but allows them to freely come to Him; Jesus gives people the opportunity to choose to live forever. God gives people the choice and teaches whoever believes and is baptized shall be saved but whosoever believeth not shall be damned. Another scripture teaches that this is the condemnation that light has come into the world and men loved darkness rather than light.

When the Angels Reap

Thus, we can explore the righteousness of the God of all creation from God making Eve from Adam's rib and calling her woman to God revealing His righteous character in power and glory through salvation in His son Jesus Christ. His power to save men and translate them out of darkness into His marvelous light was and is revealed and also His wrath against all ungodliness. God sent not His son into the world to condemn the world but that through Him the world might be saved. Like the people of Noah's generation, the scripture teaches their imaginations were only evil continually before the destruction of the world by the flood of which only eight souls were saved. The New Testament book of Romans also teaches that they became vain in their imaginations, and their foolish heart was darkened. The scripture explains just how this process happened. Romans 1: 19-23 is what happened before the imagination became vain and dark, the cause if you would of their foolish heart being darkened.

> *19.) Because that which may be known of God is manifest in them; for God hath shewed it unto them.*
>
> *20.) For the invisible things of him from the creation of the world are clearly seen, being understood by the things that are made, even his eternal power and Godhead; so that they are without excuse:*
>
> *21.) Because that, when they knew God, they glorified him not as God, neither were thankful; but became vain in their imaginations, and their foolish heart was darkened.*
>
> *22.) Professing themselves to be wise, they became fools,*
>
> *23.) And changed the glory of the uncorruptible God into an image made like to corruptible man, and to birds, and fourfooted beasts, and creeping things.*

Isn't it ironic people would see the glory and majesty and beauty of creation with the eyes that God gave them as a wonderful window to view the splendor of a sunrise against a marvelous canvas sky and then lose sight of the light of the Almighty. The light of thankfulness for the rain and food God provides, and the light of the fact the very breath and health and strength of a person depends upon God's sustaining power, by Him we live and move and have our being. The scripture warns that our eyes should be single and full of light, and if the light that be in us is darkness how great is that darkness. So, the mind's eye of how we perceive the truth and holding to the light of the truth becomes vital to walking in the light of the truth and is a major factor of whether a person will believe the truth or a lie, whether a person will do good or do evil, and whether a person will live or die.

The result of believing a lie instead of the truth and thinking themselves to be wise but in reality becoming fools which seems like at least part of the reason God actually gave them over to their own lust. So, what was the result of being turned over to their own lust? Also, what was the result of thinking themselves wise and becoming fools? How did they think themselves to be wise and become fools? Maybe we should start with the last question first and determine just how long ago this was written and inspired by God. Then we need to figure out is this state of man relevant or apparent today.

The answer of course comes directly after the statement concerning professing themselves to be wise; they became fools and changed the glory of the uncorruptible God into an image made like to corruptible man, and to birds, and fourfooted beasts, and creeping things. So, they changed the glory of the uncorruptible God into an image like to corruptible man, and to birds, and fourfooted beasts, and creeping things. Well, let's break this down piece by piece. The scripture reveals that God is uncorruptible. So, we by comparing spiritual with spiritual can examine one of many aspects of the Almighty. The scripture teaches God is a Spirit and they that worship Him must Worship Him in spirit and in truth.

Amazingly, an analogy between the flesh and the spirit quickly uncovers the problem and the solution together. The flesh is the part of man-made from the dust and corruptible, God is not a man that He should lie or the son of man that He should repent. Thus, man is susceptible to following their own fleshly nature of dust and lust of the mind, instead of following the spirit even when they know in their hearts and minds and consciences the truth that their own desires are sinful and evil and hurt other people both short term and long term as well as a person's own future. Now some may not have the knowledge of the truth but surely should understand the difference between good and evil, even as children understand when they do something wrong on purpose after they are told no, like no more cookies.

This is why the scripture teaches to know the truth and the truth shall make you free and why Jesus said "I am the way, the truth, and the life, and also told Pilate He came to bear witness of the truth of which Pilate answered what is truth. Many have sought for the truth over the ages, one of which was King Solomon. King Solomon prayed for knowledge to discern judgment after the Lord in a night vision basically asked him what he wanted. God was so pleased with Solomon's request that God blessed him greatly. The Old Testament book of Kings teaches that God revealed Himself to Solomon twice and one of those times warned Solomon not to serve other gods (idolatry). Nevertheless, Solomon had many wives and before his death he had made idols for his wives which displeased God greatly and God began to raise up enemies against Solomon and took the kingdom from him. However, God did leave one tribe the tribe of Judah for His servant David's sake who was Solomon's father. Interestingly, this concept is not isolated to one nation or city or state. In fact, it seems to be a major principle of deception negatively affecting mankind which actually leads to self-destruction through a sometimes gradual and sometimes not so gradual slope of degeneration dependent upon the rate of digression and spread of the evil device of idolatry.

So, idolatry is like a curse and a curse causeless will not come the scripture teaches. The scripture in the Old Testament spoke of different types of idolatry. Some use to take a tree, carve a piece out and cover it with gold and call it their gods, which are referred to as dumb idols. The idols cannot speak and have to be carried around and can do no good or evil because they are powerless as man's foolish devise or imagination. The bible also warns about covetousness which is idolatry. Covetousness is the act or desire of wanting what someone else has or does not belong to them.

I had not known lust unless it had been written thou shalt not covet scripture teaches about the law of God. Therefore, lust, covetousness, and idolatry are connected. The bible teaches we don't have to covet what someone else has because God shall supply all our needs according to His riches in glory. It also teaches The Lord will never leave us nor forsake us. So, we can trust in God to provide what we need and bless us with good things so we don't have to lust after evil things or things that belong to others because God can bless us with what we need. He knows what we need before we even ask scripture teaches and that every good and perfect gift comes from above from the Father of lights in whom is no variableness neither shadow of turning.

How exactly does God view sin and judgment both individually and corporately? A clue to this answer comes as a response from Jesus after the tower of Shiloam fell upon a group of people. Jesus responded suppose ye that these men were sinners above others in Jerusalem, I tell you nay but except ye repent ye shall all likewise perish. So, the Lord's view seemed much different than the people who may have thought this evil had occurred to punish those men because they must have been terrible sinners or worse sinners than those who were alive and may have thought somehow, they escaped judgment because they thought they were better or less sinful. This viewpoint may be prevalent today as well, as sometimes it may seem tempting to think well I may have sinned here and there but I'm not doing as bad as someone else I know is. So, we might seek to justify ourselves by comparing ourselves among ourselves which scripture teaches is not wise. Jesus is just and the justifier. Romans 3:26 to declare, I say, at this time his righteousness: that he might be just, and the justifier of him which believeth in Jesus.

Receive with meekness the engrafted word. James 1:21 wherefore lay apart all filthiness and superfluity of naughtiness, and receive with meekness the engrafted word, which is able to save your souls. So, another question we should consider is how does God initiate judgment, and under what circumstances might He use? The beloved king David in the Old Testament book of Samuel or Kings is an example of just how God can judge His people when His wrath is kindled against evil. 2 Samuel Chapter 24 verse 1 and again the anger of the LORD was kindled against Israel, and he moved David against them to say, Go, number Israel and Judah. 1 Chronicles Chapter 21: 1 And Satan stood up against Israel, and provoked David to number Israel. So, the same historic account one in kings and one in chronicles which reveal that He is known by the judgments which he executeth and that when His anger is kindled because of sin, wickedness, or evil doers He can remove His protection and blessing and allow people to reap the evil they have sown and without His hand of protection even satan, men, or natural disasters can be used to justly punish evil doers.

Next, since we have examined the portion of scripture "changed the glory of the uncorruptible God into an image made like to corruptible man, and to birds, and fourfooted beasts, and creeping things." We can examine the image they tried to change the image of the Holy uncorruptible God of all creation into something like to corruptible man. Interestingly, Nebuchadnezzar built an image of himself to be worshiped during the captivity of Israel and the evil leader referred to as the beast in revelation will also make an image of the beast before and attempt to force all men to worship the image paralleling Nebuchadnezzar. The next image discussed is that of birds and fourfooted beasts, and creeping things. The so-called evolutionary theory has attempted this changing the truth of God into that of apes, and some even fishes gills. So, obviously while some may be highly knowledgeable in varying subject areas, disciplines, or specialties the scripture teaches He would that none should perish but that all should come to the knowledge of the truth.

Romans 1:16-32

16.) For I am not ashamed of the gospel of Christ: for it is the power of God unto salvation to everyone that believeth; to the Jew first, and also to the Greek.

17.) For therein is the righteousness of God revealed from faith to faith: as it is written, The just shall live by faith.

18.) For the wrath of God is revealed from heaven against all ungodliness and unrighteousness of men, who hold the truth in unrighteousness;

19.) Because that which may be known of God is manifest in them; for God hath shewed it unto them.

20.) For the invisible things of him from the creation of the world are clearly seen, being understood by the things that are made, even his eternal power and Godhead; so that they are without excuse:

21.) Because that, when they knew God, they glorified him not as God, neither were thankful; but became vain in their imaginations, and their foolish heart was darkened.

22.) Professing themselves to be wise, they became fools,

23.) And changed the glory of the uncorruptible God into an image made like to corruptible man, and to birds, and fourfooted beasts, and creeping things.

24.) Wherefore God also gave them up to uncleanness through the lusts of their own hearts, to dishonour their own bodies between themselves:

25.) Who changed the truth of God into a lie, and worshipped and served the creature more than the Creator, who is blessed for ever. Amen.

26.) For this cause God gave them up unto vile affections: for even their women did change the natural use into that which is against nature:

27.) And likewise also the men, leaving the natural use of the woman, burned in their lust one toward another; men with men working that which is unseemly, and receiving in themselves that recompence of their error which was meet.

28.) And even as they did not like to retain God in their knowledge, God gave them over to a reprobate mind, to do those things which are not convenient;

> 29.) *Being filled with all unrighteousness, fornication, wickedness, covetousness, maliciousness; full of envy, murder, debate, deceit, malignity; whisperers,*
>
> 30.) *Backbiters, haters of God, despiteful, proud, boasters, inventors of evil things, disobedient to parents,*
>
> 31.) *Without understanding, covenantbreakers, without natural affection, implacable, unmerciful:*
>
> 32.) *Who knowing the judgment of God, that they which commit such things are worthy of death, not only do the same, but have pleasure in them that do them.*

Romans 1: 24 wherefore God also gave them up to uncleanness through the lusts of their own hearts, to dishonour their own bodies between themselves:

The scripture teaches it is a fearful thing to fall into the hands of the living God. In this case, the danger of God letting people fighting to get out of His hand becomes exceedingly dangerous as the result of God giving people over to their own desires can mean their own destruction at their own hands by their own devices. The aids virus is one such example of the terrible self-inflicting wounds of dishonouring their own bodies which God gave to mankind. The scripture is very clear we are the temple of God and if we defile the temple, God will destroy it. The CDC aids report history reveals the 1980 discovery of aids which at the time puzzled the medical community. The results of early reports from large cities on the east and west coast quickly revealed that one hundred percent of the early cases were directly linked to Sodomy. An old sin reappearing in modern times under a new guise of terminologies all of which have the same sad spiritual result if not repented of and that result is sickness and death. The aids epidemic has killed multiplied millions and has spread to affect many innocent children who contracted the disease at birth or through botched blood transfusions. Thus, sodomy causes aids and is a terrible health hazard. So, why are some politicians supporting groups and a small portion of the population who are promoting aids causing acts against nature when the CDC reports clearly state the dangers of sodomy and the aids virus? The answer seems to evidently be for a small percentage of a voting group even though the practice can kill those who practice it. God's word is clear that He is merciful and loving so repent and turn to God before it is too late, be reconciled to God.

> 25.) *Who changed the truth of God into a lie, and worshipped and served the creature more than the Creator, who is blessed for ever. Amen.*

The next part of Romans explains the negative effects of people dishonoring their bodies and then the consequences of such defilement which result in changing the truth of God into lie. This has been witnessed over the centuries in the western hemisphere and expanding much further into some cultures, laws, and learning institutions through a so-called humanistic world view. A falsehood in the very term of the word human which was coined hundreds of years ago in rebellion against the view of God's creation of man in His image to turn the truth of God into a lie by calling man human or ape man. The reason at the time involved the context of the people losing confidence in the corrupted Catholic Church of the Middle Ages in Europe. Iniquity caused a negative perspective even though the Protestant movement outlined the deviation away from the holy scriptural instruction and guidance as the cause of the corruptions. However, those who maybe didn't join the Protestant movement out of fear of reprisal or just chose a life contrary to truth because they were or became offended by the many abuses of the corrupted Catholic Church during the inquisition. A time period which reported many innocent people being falsely accused of heresy and put to death for disagreeing with church authority which had power and governing authority.

Who changed the truth of God into a lie, and worshipped and served the creature more than the Creator, who is blessed forever. Amen. This verse also seems to ring obvious in our generation as people seek to change the truth of God into a lie and worship the creature more than the creator in many confused and defiant ways like is seen in men dressing like women and saying they are women. The scripture teaches this is the condemnation that light has come into the world and men loved darkness rather than light. The good news is Jesus died for our sins so we could turn from them and be free; be reconciled to God.

> 26.) *For this cause God gave them up unto vile affections: for even their women did change the natural use into that which is against nature:*
>
> 27.) *And likewise also the men, leaving the natural use of the woman, burned in their lust one toward another; men with men working that which is unseemly, and receiving in themselves that recompence of their error which was meet.*

The dangers of sin and rebellion against God are like forsaking one's own mercy. The dangers of being so blind to sin by the lust of this world are that the lust of the world is not of the Father but of the world. The Father God and Jesus Christ His son created all things including and of course that includes mankind. The Father and Lord Jesus created man in His image and in His righteousness. Therefore, God is holy, that is His character, so His creation is expected to be like Him, to be holy as He is holy. So, mankind should be like their creator, Godly, righteous, loving, and merciful. The adversary, the devil, however, is against God and His creation that is made in His image, who the devil would love to steal, kill, and destroy. The devil is doomed because pride was found in his heart against the Almighty. The devil knows the truth very well and is evilly wise to twist and pervert the truth to seek to deceive man in an attempt to turn them from God their creator. The devil knows his judgment has been set for the lake of fire as told in the book of revelation. Therefore, if he can't destroy God's creation because of God's mercy toward them, he will try and get them to destroy themselves.

1 Corinthians 3:17 If any man defile the temple of God, him shall God destroy; for the temple of God is holy, which temple ye are.

God will send one angel to bind satan in revelation to be thrown into the bottomless pit, and there is no wisdom against God. This is why we need to cry out for knowledge, wisdom, and understanding, and if we are sinning against God by lust or evil to repent now before it is too late. He doesn't take pleasure in the legs of a man or the strength of the horse, but in those who trust in His mercy. Though hand join in hand they shall not be unpunished the scripture explains so thinking because many may have forsaken the way that maybe an individual or group of people or even government entity can join forces against the Almighty would be a vain and quickly fleeting thought especially on the day of judgement. The nations are like grasshoppers, a drop in the bucket, and less than nothing to the Creator.

God has no respect of persons so the same God who executed righteous judgment in days of old in generations past will surely execute righteous judgment on this generation. He loves judgment and mercy rejoiceth against judgment, and His mercy endureth forever. He is longsuffering toward us not willing that any should parish but all should come to the knowledge of the truth. Therefore, the Almighty is being patient for the precious fruit of the earth. The wicked will never see light again if they leave this world and have not received the love of the truth. Jesus is the way, the truth, and the life, and no man can come to the Father but by Him. The bible teaches of a place of judgment where the worm dieth not, so people who choose darkness instead of life will likely always remember the day and opportunity God gave them to accept Jesus as their savior and to escape this present evil world and be delivered from sin and death and hell, or eventually the lake of fire.

So, if a man chooses the pleasures of sin for a season the scripture is clear there is still no peace to the wicked and we reap what we sow, and there will be a fearful looking for of judgment to the wicked, and the way of the transgressor is hard. Even after all the tribulation for loving darkness and sin over a loving savior God may still reach out to save and redeem a repentant heart, or hear the prayers of loved one's seeking for the persons soul. The bible is clear hell enlarges itself daily and that the smoke of their torment will ascend up forever and ever before the saints and the holy angels. If a person chooses to follow the lust of this world, they may not even realize they are following the devil or allowing the devil to lead them right into the pits of hell never to see light again, never to see a small glimmer of hope again, never to stop suffering again as death and hell will be cast into the lake of fire where the beast, false prophet, and satan will suffer for ever and ever along with those who chose fleshly, temporary lust, as the body over just a few decades will generally decay in weakness of flesh anyway.

Romans 1: 28 and even as they did not like to retain God in their knowledge, God gave them over to a reprobate mind, to do those things which are not convenient;

The conscience is a powerful part of the inward man which God created in the body soul and spirit man. The soul or psuche in Greek and the pnuema for spirit give reference to the internal workings of mankind. Titus 1:15 unto the pure all things are pure: but unto them that are defiled, and unbelieving is nothing pure; but even their mind and conscience is defiled. The scripture illustrates this in another area when discussing the eternal state of men's souls. The scripture teaches fear not them who can kill the body and after that can do nothing but fear Him who hath power to destroy both body and soul in hell. Yet again, the scripture discusses a situation where some would not accept deliverance from possible tribulations or death that they might obtain a better resurrection referring to deliverance from death.

The first part of Romans 1: 28 explains that they did not like to retain God in their knowledge. So, the conscience knowledge of God inside the people God created turned away from their own knowledge internally and in their minds to try and not keep or retain God in their thoughts. So, God who gave man the ability to know and understand is now being ignored because of wicked works the people were committing. Therefore, the second part of the scripture goes on to explain what happens when men try to push God out of their knowledge, minds, and life's. The people were sort of granted their own desires to be separated from the loving God who made them, died for their sins, and made a way for them to live forever with Him in heaven and the new heaven and the new earth scripture reveals.

The second part also goes on to explain how God gave them over to a reprobate mind, to do those things which are not convenient. A mind without righteous principle or guidance, a mind perverted and twisted, a mind given over to commit whatever evil their mind could sink to without any profit or good. This was the mind reprobate and wicked similar to those in the days of Sodom and Gomorrah who had given themselves over unto fornication. Instead of ordinate affection, agape love of God, and the love of God saving people from darkness, these people chose and may today choose to follow their own lust of evil rather than true principles of God's love for others, family, and righteousness by faith in Jesus Christ. People should quickly turn from their own ways, sins, and evil, and be reconciled to God who can deliver them from evil and the snare of the devil attempting to deceive them to follow the devils devices to try and get them to voluntarily destroy their own lives, and worst of all condemn their own souls to hell and the second death the lake of fire where satan himself is set to go. Unless they turn to the truth and fear Gods judgment and receive God's mercy to be justified by the faith of His son Jesus Christ and cleansed from their evil ways and works by Jesus' blood and believing Jesus is the Son of the living God and be saved and delivered from the clutches of the devil.

> *29.) Being filled with all unrighteousness, fornication, wickedness, covetousness, maliciousness; full of envy, murder, debate, deceit, malignity; whisperers,*
>
> *30.) Backbiters, haters of God, despiteful, proud, boasters, inventors of evil things, disobedient to parents,*
>
> *31.) Without understanding, covenantbreakers, without natural affection, implacable, unmerciful:*
>
> *32.) Who knowing the judgment of God, that they which commit such things are worthy of death, not only do the same, but have pleasure in them that do them.*

The last section of Romans 1: 29-32 reveals the works of a reprobate mind or like in Galatians 5 the lust of the flesh. The far opposite of the fruits of the Spirit which should live and dwell within the hearts and minds and life's of those who have asked the Lord for forgiveness, not of our own works are we saved but by God's mercy. Jesus, He who was and Is and Is to come, died for the sins of the whole world for all have sinned and fall short of the glory of God so His great love wherewith He loved us extended and extends to all the world.

Therefore, His grace is open for you to enter into the door by faith and receive Jesus into your heart and life and be reconciled to God. The scripture teaches that if any man be in Christ, He is a new creature, old things have passed away behold all things have been made new. The angels rejoice over one sinner who comes to repentance. Imagine how great you will feel on the inside knowing you are completely clean from sin. Your sins washed away by the blood of Jesus Christ the son of God who made atonement for our sins. You can have peace like you may have never even known just by giving your life to the Savior. The scripture teaching is clear that if we save our life we will lose it, but if we lose our life for His sake we will save it. So, be ye reconciled to God.

The bible teaches some about the appearance of Jesus Christ the Lord our Savior. It describes in Isaiah how He would be like the root out of dry ground and that there was no comeliness in Him. The scripture talks about how they plucked the Saviors beard. The scripture also speaks in revelation of Jesus' glorified appearance. (13.) And in the midst of the seven candlesticks one like unto the Son of man, clothed with a garment down to the foot, and girt about the paps with a golden girdle. (14.) His head and his hairs were white like wool, as white as snow; and his eyes were as a flame of fire; (15.) And his feet like unto fine brass, as if they burned in a furnace; and his voice as the sound of many waters. (16.) And he had in his right hand seven stars: and out of his mouth went a sharp twoedged sword: and his countenance was as the sun shineth in his strength.

The Bible teaches those who are redeemed by the blood of Jesus Christ our Savior that we are sealed with the Holy Spirit until the redemption of the purchased possession and we shall be like him. The bible also teaches that the saints will live forever and that they will not be hurt by the second death (lake of fire). Again, the scripture teaches like a seed the body is buried a natural body in weakness and is raised a spiritual body in power and it does not yet appear what we shall be. The suffering of this present time does not compare with the glory that shall be revealed in us and to be absent from the body is to be present with the Lord. Romans 8: 19 for the earnest expectation of the creature waiteth for the manifestation of the sons of God. 20 For the creature was made subject to vanity, not willingly, but by reason of him who hath subjected the same in hope, 21 Because the creature itself also shall be delivered from the bondage of corruption into the glorious liberty of the children of God. 22 For we know that the whole creation groaneth and travaileth in pain together until now. 23 And not only they, but ourselves also, which have the firstfruits of the Spirit, even we ourselves groan within ourselves, waiting for the adoption, to wit, the redemption of our body.

2 Thessalonians 2:1-17

> *1 Now we beseech you, brethren, by the coming of our Lord Jesus Christ, and by our gathering together unto him,*
>
> *2 That ye be not soon shaken in mind, or be troubled, neither by spirit, nor by word, nor by letter as from us, as that the day of Christ is at hand.*
>
> *3 Let no man deceive you by any means: for that day shall not come, except there come a falling away first, and that man of sin be revealed, the son of perdition;*

4 *Who opposeth and exalteth himself above all that is called God, or that is worshipped; so that he as God sitteth in the temple of God, shewing himself that he is God.*

5 *Remember ye not, that, when I was yet with you, I told you these things?*

6 *And now ye know what withholdeth that he might be revealed in his time.*

7 *For the mystery of iniquity doth already work: only he who now letteth will let, until he be taken out of the way.*

8 *And then shall that Wicked be revealed, whom the Lord shall consume with the spirit of his mouth, and shall destroy with the brightness of his coming:*

9 *Even him, whose coming is after the working of Satan with all power and signs and lying wonders,*

10 *And with all deceivableness of unrighteousness in them that perish; because they received not the love of the truth, that they might be saved.*

11 *And for this cause God shall send them strong delusion, that they should believe a lie:*

12 *That they all might be damned who believed not the truth, but had pleasure in unrighteousness.*

13 *But we are bound to give thanks alway to God for you, brethren beloved of the Lord, because God hath from the beginning chosen you to salvation through sanctification of the Spirit and belief of the truth:*

14 *Whereunto he called you by our gospel, to the obtaining of the glory of our Lord Jesus Christ.*

15 *Therefore, brethren, stand fast, and hold the traditions which ye have been taught, whether by word, or our epistle.*

16 *Now our Lord Jesus Christ himself, and God, even our Father, which hath loved us, and hath given us everlasting consolation and good hope through grace,*

17 *Comfort your hearts, and stablish you in every good word and work.*

Great empires throughout time, some of which reached pinnacles of vast parts of the world and peoples, like the mighty Roman Empire which was in authority in the earthly realm when Jesus dwelt in Israel around the time of His death, burial, resurrection, and ascension. The Roman Emperors probably felt untouchable in the dominant eras of their kingdoms on earth. They likely lived in the splendor of wealth and innovations of their times like they would live on forever as they may have felt their empires would. However, the bible teaches about men who return to dust and who before they die leave their names on their lands as if they would continue on earth forever. The people in their seemingly powerful state may have felt they answered to no one and their judgments were more upright than others or who could stop them if they were unrighteous because they had power to do according to their own minds.

However, over time the scriptures just become more absolutely true when realized over the ages to peoples who read the history of great empires that they too soon pass away and no one really remembers them anymore, or places too much thought on them because of the concerns and times people are currently in. However, a wise man may certainly learn from such great empires and kings and kingdoms of ages gone by to discover that being right in one's own eyes is brief as life is like a vapor. If the peoples of ancient kingdoms who died in their sins in a wicked state in rebellion against God could return though Jesus' parable tells otherwise, would they give the same sad scenario of the rich man who lifted his eyes being in torment in hell. The rich man was told there was a great gulf fixed and that if they did not believe the prophets they would not believe even if one went back from the dead to tell them not to come to that horrible place.

The great Egyptian empire after Joseph the patriarch, Jacob's son, was one of the most powerful on earth of that time and in many generations a strong nation. The leaders felt the children of Israel were becoming too strong and turned to evil and wickedness against a people who were innocent and blessed by Almighty God. The fear of the children of Israel caused Egyptian leaders to device an evil plan to kill the firstborn of Israel in an attempt to weaken them. They may have justified their murderous acts by feeling they were preserving their own power or controlling overpopulating. They may have thought they were helping end suffering by not needing to feed more children which would give more for the rich and powerful of that day, more land and less people to have to provide housing and work for which could impinge upon their luxurious lifestyles of ease and comfort, or maybe they felt less trouble for them to have to deal with social problems.

Isn't it sad the attempts to justify abortion today when many of the extremely wealthy have had their family or they themselves in major positions of leadership in these killing zone organizations like so called T.O.D.E. (Terminology of Death and Evil) planned parenthood? This would make likely attempts to cover their true motives and intentions for the evil harming of innocent children for big money under the guise of planning and even more ridiculously the word parent involved when that too is falsehood because they are destroying people's opportunities to even be parents. Similarly, the terrible falsehood and health hazard of sodomy but on one major activist organizations own website they discuss help for aids (T.O.D.E.) when sodomy was the one hundred percent cause of aids related deaths in the 1980's when it was first discovered in predominately large cities. The aids virus is still also a major epidemic which has killed multiplied millions of people and many innocent people through inadvertent blood transfusions and even with medications is a major health hazard to today's innocent children. Nevertheless, many are targeting the youth for such perversions when youth in schools were under federal law required to only teach abstinence which the CDC advises because it is the safest lifestyle for protecting children and their futures. Moreover, the main activists group concerning the promotion of sodomy was also connected to a pedophile group in the seventies called man boy love. The wickedness and deception is very prevalent, attacking the innocent children either through killing innocent healthy children for profit or through seductively attempting to pervert with the intent to abuse innocent children. The baby killing multi-million dollar non-for-profit decided they weren't getting away with enough tax payer funding of their evil work so they then were caught selling baby body parts for profit and in a federal court actually admitted to killing a baby born alive and after taking a part of the baby. This is genocide of the innocent and it is supposed to be illegal for tax payers to fund abortion, and even more illegal to profit from illegal selling of innocent and healthy baby body parts under the guise (T.O.D.E.) of so called medical progress (repugnant degradation).

The German Empire was also one of the mighty empires in history. The Germanic tribes actually laid the early defeats to the weakening structure of the Western Roman Empire. The German empire then amassed great armies and forces and led many nations spiraling into major world wars in modern history. Germany's aggression before World War II went unchecked by other nations who chose appeasement rather than accountability for breaking the treaty of Versailles after the first world conflict. Nevertheless, maybe the biggest shock of all was the internal workings of the German leadership to manipulate their own people by taking over churches and spreading propaganda to control the masses. These leaders guided military forces and secret policing agencies to terrorize people who stood for the truth against tyranny like the famous German preacher who stood against the propaganda.

The German leadership and its cronies had become so vile in their own attempts to prove they were the chosen race and Germanize the world they began to attack innocent Jewish people. The horrific scars of the holocaust should serve as a warning against evil empires who feel their military strength or technological advancement make them untouchably empowered to destroy innocent lives for their own twisted agendas. Germany and Japan led the way in technological advancement and warfare of its time with some of the most prolific researchers developing cutting edge innovations for military aircraft, submarines, and resources. The youth were trained for military activities under the name of their national leader. Germany likely had some of the most knowledgeable physicians and sophisticated health care of their day but without strong righteous moral guidance, but actually the opposite, destructive guidance from teachings from a prominent German around the fifteen hundreds which taught evil against God's chosen people, the Jewish nation.

These medical and technological advancements soon turned into wicked mistreatment through terrible experiments on people while they were awake and without anesthesia. The systematic hunting and organized effort to find, persecute, torture, and kill millions of innocent men, woman, and children. Innocent woman and children were sent to the gas chambers or starved to death while working or shot and abused under terrible conditions. These people committing these terrible unthinkable atrocities on innocent people were highly intelligent and being led by perpetrators willing to deceive their own people by covering what they were doing or misleading them through propaganda to passively stand by or even more troubling actively engage in the killing of innocent people because of twisted ideologies and principles like only the strong survive evolutionary lies.

Does this sound similar to what is happening today? Where the majority of people likely oppose such evil surmising by small percentages of the population who support murdering babies on demand or promoting sodomy or the defilement of trying to mutilate the bodies of children when verbal abuse can be considered abuse of a child, much less the reputable manipulation of impressionable innocent children. Children who develop mentally wouldn't even be taught secondary anatomy and physiology are being targeted like one seven-year-old Texas boy whose father fights for his son just to live his childhood in peace and activist mommy who wants to chemically castrate her son in the name of insane perverted wickedness and lawyers were able to change judges to get an activist judge of their liking to give mom control over the dad.

Moreover, current legislation in the U.S. Congress is seeking to advance sodomy over the first amendment in an attempt to force the majority of Christian people in a nation founded on Christian Judeo principles to accept unconscionable principles of sin by a small percentage of the population. Ludicrous and delusional are terms that come to mind when examining the facts surrounding such legislative tyranny. Especially in light of the fact that some in the field of psychology are deceptively and subtly suggesting the Q in the T.O.D.E. (Terminology of Death and Evil) actually involves a list of perversions, one of which is pedophilia under the guise of what one of their lead groups calls attractions to minors, wicked,

wicked, wicked. Slowly attempting to desensitize following the initial shock of completely evil intentions toward innocent children is mildly introduced through a systematic concerted effort to gradually propagandize people to think nothing is really wrong with raping and abusing innocent young people.

The alike has been seen with groups seeking to lower the age of consent as was led by a sodomite and passed in California. The age of consent was lowered under the guise of not wanting to put people on the sex offender status. So, now in California a fourteen-year-old can be coerced and raped under the law by adults as long as they somehow gave consent. Even though most states probably don't even consider minors developmentally able to give consent because of their age and being impressionable to where adults could easily coerce a child or minor. Will God not bring righteous judgment upon such evil? Does God not see the evil being perpetrated upon the young innocent? The scripture teaches who will stand up against the evil doers. Will the righteous arise? Are we in the days of whosoever 'will let will let', and as taught in revelations "let them be wicked still" because the judgment is currently or so close at hand? Will God hold Christians accountable if they join or promote killing or abusing the innocent in any way?

Do the dead cry out from the pits of hell that rejected Christ and hurt young innocent lives in the 1940's or 60's or 80's not to make the same mistakes while maybe feeling like we are living a life of ease or convenience that could cause us to turn a blind eye to hurting the innocent? Will the modern conveniences of our day force our hand because we feel the great comforts of technology so big tech and huge companies get wealthy off of Christian consumers and then turn around and persecute them with the millions or even billions of dollars of merchandise they sold to Christians to the point some feel boycotting is no longer effective because not enough will unite to stop buying products from companies who use their money to promote the killing of innocent babies and sodomy while discriminating against and targeting Christian businesses who stand for biblical truth? Will Christians unite to promote only wholesome Christian values taught by the Savior and His holy Word? Will Christians take time to research and find Christian businesses to buy from and spend their money on products from companies who care about Christian principles and people? Be ye reconciled to God.

The scripture teaches to redeem the time because the days are evil. The bible also teaches about a time of great tribulation which will hit the earth like has never been experienced before. This tribulation period discussed in the holy text involves a leader referred to as the beast that will forecast devices and by peace destroy many. A very interesting part of the scenario is that the beast will forsake the holy covenant, and many will betray the holy covenant because of flattery. The beast will subsequentially or at some point exalt himself above all that is called God or that is worshiped. The scripture is clear concerning a falling away must first happen and the love of many shall wax cold because of iniquity. On the other hand, the saints will be doing exploits and instructing many. The scripture also speaks of the dragon sending out a flood to destroy God's chosen but the earth will swallow up the waters which indicates divine protection even though some of the righteous will fall to try some of the others and make them white. The scripture also is clear that a time will come which Daniel spoke of that they will wear out the saints. Nevertheless, the hope in Daniel is also revealed through the scriptural teaching that the saints will possess the kingdom.

The good news is that God's lovingkindness is new every morning. The good news is Jesus is going to reign for a thousand years in Jerusalem after the beast and the false prophet are cast into the lake of fire and the dragon, satan, that ole serpent will be cast into the bottomless pit for a thousand years. The first resurrection the saints will enjoy and not be hurt by the second death. After the thousand years satan will be loosed from the bottomless pit and will gather Gog and Magog and encamp about the holy city Jerusalem, and God will send fire to destroy. The great white throne judgment will be set, and the books will be open of the works that have been done whether good or bad to be judged for their works.

The Lamb's book of life will also be before the judgement throne and whosoever's names are not written in the lambs book of life shall be cast into the lake of fire. Be reconciled to God today and ask Jesus to forgive you of your sins and come into your heart and save you. Jesus loves you and died for you and is offering you eternal life, be reconciled to God today by faith in Jesus Christ the son of God the Holy Father. The Lord is righteous in all His ways and holy in all His works, His righteousness endureth forever and there is no unrighteousness in Him. He is holy and He is perfect, and He is full of grace and truth. All praise, glory, and honour be to the Holy one of Israel who is great and greatly to be praised for He is the Mighty God of Jacob.

Isaiah 44:6-9

> 6.) *Thus saith the LORD the King of Israel, and his redeemer the LORD of hosts; I am the first, and I am the last; and beside me there is no God.*
>
> 7.) *And who, as I, shall call, and shall declare it, and set it in order for me, since I appointed the ancient people? and the things that are coming, and shall come, let them shew unto them.*

8.) *Fear ye not, neither be afraid: have not I told thee from that time, and have declared it? ye are even my witnesses. Is there a God beside me? yea, there is no God; I know not any.*

9.) *They that make a graven image are all of them vanity; and their delectable things shall not profit; and they are their own witnesses; they see not, nor know; that they may be ashamed.*

Of course, a culture is not bigger than God not the errors of culture of one nation or group of people within a nation or even nations. The scripture is very certain that there is no God beside the God of Abraham, Isaac, and Jacob. The God and Father of the Lord Jesus Christ is the son of God, He who was and is and is to come. Verse seven asks an important question for all people to consider today especially in the light that no man can keep alive his own soul which means if a person is still living there is hope for God to have mercy. The verse asks who "And who, as I, shall call, and shall declare it, and set it in order for me, since I appointed the ancient people? and the things that are coming, and shall come, let them shew unto them." So, we should ask ourselves who like God has ordained the ancient people from thence till now and to come. In other words, God's predeterminate counsel from the beginning.

The genealogy from Adam to Seth and the eventual judgment of the flood upon the descendants of Cain was an early evidence of God's ordering of events. Jacob and Esau before they were born it was determined that the elder would serve the younger while the children were in the womb and had not done good or evil. Of course, He revealed the truth and it happened just as it was proclaimed. David was a king after God's own heart chosen and elect with faithfulness and God's amazing grace being revealed generations before his birth. The history of King David can be traced back to the book of Ruth in the Old Testament which provides a powerful insight into the appointing of ancient people.

Naomi a mother who lost her husband and sons to early deaths after moving into a strange land found comfort from Ruth her daughter in law who refused to leave her mother-in-law after her husband had died. Ruth followed Naomi back to Israel when Naomi felt she had lost everything and maybe even felt abandoned by God. Ruth was a faithful woman and was shown mercy by a powerful man of God in Israel named Boaz. Boaz later redeemed Ruth by marrying her and they had a child who would become the great grandfather of King David. The grace of God revealed through a Moabite woman who loved a mother in Israel became a chosen vessel to become part of God's master plan to bring forth the savior into the world. King Jesus was brought into this world through the lineage of a woman named Ruth, who exemplifies how God looks upon the hurting and those who love and care for those who have been hurt like she did. She gave up her life to help her mother-in-law and God gave her so much more.

God has no respect of persons or cultural movement even though he may honor a movement if it is found in His righteousness. This is why one should diligently consider a cause before delving into it in case the motives or actions do not bring glory and honor to the one true God. The Old Testament of the Holy Scriptures teaches one should speak the truth and stand for the truth even if an assembly or crowd or group may be supporting a lie. Some in the crowd may be confused and not fully understand the situation or the cause and some may desire contention because of ulterior motives and seek to deceive others to join their rebellion. However, the truth will not change and God is not moved by fear of man or groups or organizations or military strength as the strength of the horse is a vain thing in the day of battle if the Lord is not on your side or you are not on His side.

God's judgment will rest in righteousness and the righteous will see their desire upon the wicked. Jesus seemed to have lost the final battle as the chief priests and some rulers mocked Him on the cross. Herod likely felt strong and confident after he killed the righteous prophet John the Baptist and the apostle James with the sword and saw that it pleased the people. Where are those people who mocked Jesus at now? The scripture teaches that for the joy set before Him, He endured the cross. The scripture declared many years before that Jesus would be resurrected and Jesus proclaimed that He would rise after three days well before it happened so when it happened, they would believe. The tomb sits empty but what about the chief priests and those who mocked the Lord? What happened to king Herod? He was struck by the angel of the Lord after not giving God glory when the people cried like Herod was a God and the worms ate him. Whose report will we believe?

Why does it matter whose report we believe? The reason it matters is if we believe the report of the Lord, we will believe the truth of God's word and His word is forever settled in the heavens. The scripture also teaches to let God's word be true and every man a liar. In other words, even if the majority decided to not believe the report of the Lord, they would all be found liars before the living God who created them in the first place. This is why the bible speaks of men forsaking their own mercy and being turned to vanity. The wonderful thing about believing the report of the Lord is that in the latter days ("For I know that my redeemer liveth, and that he shall stand at the latterday upon the earth:" Job 19:25, KJV) it will be well with those who believed His report for all things work together to the good of them who love God and who are the called according to His purpose.

So, when a person believes the report of the Lord by faith they join the loving and caring family of God and enter into the door of God's perfect will and purpose for their lives. This is why all things work together for good to them who love God because He is able to change circumstances and align situations over time to ensure His purpose is completed. On the contrary, if a person has an evil heart of unbelief about their Creator and believes someone else's report that is in contrast with the truth of God, then they are choosing to be led astray or follow their own way.

One scripture puts it something like this; the turning away of the simple and the prosperity of fools shall slay them, and those by whom the way of truth is evil spoken of. So, some and depending upon the time in history and or the generation even many may be led to believe a false report. This does not catch the Master by surprise as He knows those who are His, and Jesus also knew those who did not believe amongst the crowds who followed Him as He fed thousands, healed many of sicknesses and diseases, and delivered people from evil spirits making them free.

Of course, all have sinned and fall short of the glory of God which is why Jesus appeared at the end of times to redeem men from their trespasses and sins by His own blood for without the shedding of blood there is no remission of sins. God is a just and righteous judge and requires justice and judgment. The Old Testament makes this clear in the book of Deuteronomy when the requirements of obedience are discussed for receiving the blessing of the Lord and the consequences of disobedience to the laws of God which bring curses. Incredibly, by the mercy of Jesus, Jesus became a curse for us in order to redeem people from the curse for cursed is everyone who is hanged upon a tree.

The Lord is also very patient and waits for souls who may come to Him for salvation either in their early years, middle years, or in old age. He also saves when people may be about to take their last breath or go into a fierce battle. The thief on the cross asked Jesus to remember him when He came into His kingdom and Jesus told the man today you will be with me in paradise. Isn't that quite amazing that those few words and Jesus realized the once thief had a change of heart and wanted Jesus to remember Him. Oh, the love of Jesus our righteous savior extending to people in the waning moments of time. The scripture teaches I can't judge others, others can's judge me, I can't even judge myself, and not judge anything before it's time for God will judge every man's work of what sort it is in His appointed time. God's hand is not short that it cannot save. This is why we cannot judge because God can deal with a person's heart and mind and translate them from darkness into His marvelous light.

Amazing Grace who saved a wretch like me referring to the scripture verse which teaches oh what a wretched man that I am who shall deliver me from the body of this death. The battle between the lust of the flesh and mind (carnal mindedness) works of the flesh and the walking after the Spirit of God (spiritually minded) which is life and peace often rage in the soul of man. The fleshly lusts war for temporary evil pleasures while the works of the spirit lead to love, joy, peace, longsuffering, gentleness, meekness, kindness against such there is not law. So, the daily decisions to believe the report of the Lord and to commit to His ways and walk after the Spirit lead to everlasting life through faith in Jesus Christ.

While the lusts of the flesh like adultery and fornication, murders, envies, reveling and such like shall not inherit the kingdom of God because the flesh will return to the dust so if a man serves evil fleshly desires, they will sow to the works of the flesh and reap corruption. So, when a person leaves this world having been dead to God Spiritually because they chose to live for the lust of their flesh their flesh will go to dust but because they believed not the report of the Lord the spiritual death will lead them to separation from God in hell and at the judgment the lake of fire for eternity which is the second death.

The time is so short like a vapor for such immense Spiritual consequences upon the souls of men. Please don't wait if you read this warning, please heed the truth and believe the report of the Lord and be reconciled to God before it is too late. The bible teaches the enemy will rejoice over the multitudes he has brought down to the sides of the pit in hell. Don't let anyone take your crown and one day glory over you that you followed them into hell and torment because they hated God or were so blinded by lust in their own hearts that they denied God. Let your life be forever free in God's love and mercy and in His eternal kingdom with everlasting joy on your head when you awake from sleep in death or the Master returns and will he find faith on the earth instead of awaking to everlasting contempt knowing their will only be utter darkness, suffering, weeping and gnashing of teeth.

Daniel 12:2 and many of them that sleep in the dust of the earth shall awake, some to everlasting life, and some to shame and everlasting contempt.

(Image above: solvechurchproblems.com)

Jesus: He Who Is, Who was, and Who Is to Come

(Image above: relevancy22.blogspot.com)

(Image above: christiantruthcenter.com)

(Image above: goacsundayschool.blogspot.com)

Chosen

I John 2

28.) And now, little children, abide in him; that, when he shall appear, we may have confidence, and not be ashamed before him at his coming.

29.) If ye know that he is righteous, ye know that every one that doeth righteousness is born of him.

Imagine awaking to everlasting life in the presence of the Lord and the holy angels. How magnificent the sights and sounds of glory land. One song writer penned the beautiful words to Beulah Land. Several places in the Holy Scriptures it discusses the glorious splendor of this divine heavenly dwelling place and those who have been justified to be there. One such place of the later is in the book of **Hebrews chapter twelve** where it teaches about the spirits of just men made perfect. 22.) But ye are come unto mount Sion, and unto the city of the living God, the heavenly Jerusalem, and to an innumerable company of angels, 23.) To the general assembly and church of the firstborn, which are written in heaven, and to God the Judge of all, and to the spirits of just men made perfect, 24.) And to Jesus the mediator of the new covenant, and to the blood of sprinkling, that speaketh better things than that of Abel. 25.) See that ye refuse not him that speaketh. For if they escaped not who refused him that spake on earth, much more shall not we escape, if we turn away from him that speaketh from heaven:

The bible, the Word of God, also gives insight into the heavenly realm through the Apostle Paul's description of a man whether in the body or out the body he knew not, but such an one was carried into the third heaven. **2 Corinthians 12:** 1.) it is not expedient for me doubtless to glory. I will come to visions and revelations of the Lord. 2.) I knew a man in Christ above fourteen years ago, (whether in the body, I cannot tell; or whether out of the body, I cannot tell: God knoweth;) such an one caught up to the third heaven. 3.) And I knew such a man, (whether in the body, or out of the body, I cannot tell: God knoweth;) 4.) How that he was caught up into paradise, and heard unspeakable words, which it is not lawful for a man to utter. 5.) Of such an one will I glory: yet of myself I will not glory, but in mine infirmities.

So, what does paradise look like? What will the New Jerusalem look like? What will it be like in the world to come; the new heaven and the new earth which God is preparing for those who believe and trust in Him? Abraham was called the friend of God, and the father of faith. The bible clearly teaches that Abraham believed God and it was accounted to him for righteousness. The scripture also clearly teaches in Romans four of the New Testament that the promise to Abraham and to his seed was by grace through faith and not the works of the law. The law was a schoolmaster to bring us to Christ for if there had been a law that could have brought salvation then salvation might have come through the law. Nevertheless, Jesus, Emmanuel, the son of God, was born of a virgin and came to take away the sins of the world and bring salvation to all people, whosoever believeth in Him shall not perish but have everlasting life.

Isaiah 65: 9 And I will bring forth a seed out of Jacob, and out of Judah an inheritor of my mountains: and mine elect shall inherit it, and my servants shall dwell there. 10.) And Sharon shall be a fold of flocks, and the valley of Achor a place for the herds to lie down in, for my people that have sought me. 11.) But ye are they that forsake the LORD, that forget my holy mountain, that prepare a table for that troop, and that furnish the drink offering unto that number. 12.) Therefore will I number you to the sword, and ye shall all bow down to the slaughter: because when I called, ye did not answer; when I spake, ye did not hear; but did evil before mine eyes, and did choose that wherein I delighted not. 13.) Therefore thus saith the Lord GOD, Behold, my servants shall eat, but ye shall be hungry: behold, my servants shall drink, but ye shall be thirsty: behold, my servants shall rejoice, but ye shall be ashamed: 14.) Behold, my servants shall sing for joy of heart, but ye shall cry for sorrow of heart, and shall howl for vexation of spirit. 15.) And ye shall leave your name for a curse unto my chosen: for the Lord GOD shall slay thee, and call his servants by another name: 16.) That he who blesseth himself in the earth shall bless himself in the God of truth; and he that sweareth in the earth shall swear by the God of truth; because the former troubles are forgotten, and because they are hid from mine eyes. **17.) For, behold, I create new heavens and a new earth: and the former shall not be remembered, nor come into mind.** 18.) But be ye glad and rejoice forever in that which I create: for, behold, I create Jerusalem a rejoicing, and her people a joy. 19.) And I will rejoice in

Jerusalem, and joy in my people: and the voice of weeping shall be no more heard in her, nor the voice of crying. 20.) There shall be no more thence an infant of days, nor an old man that hath not filled his days: for the child shall die an hundred years old; but the sinner being an hundred years old shall be accursed.

Revelation 21:1 And I saw a new heaven and a new earth: for the first heaven and the first earth were passed away; and there was no more sea. 2.) And I John saw the holy city, new Jerusalem, coming down from God out of heaven, prepared as a bride adorned for her husband. 3.) And I heard a great voice out of heaven saying, Behold, the tabernacle of God is with men, and he will dwell with them, and they shall be his people, and God himself shall be with them, and be their God. 4.) And God shall wipe away all tears from their eyes; and there shall be no more death, neither sorrow, nor crying, neither shall there be any more pain: for the former things are passed away. 5.) And he that sat upon the throne said, Behold, I make all things new. And he said unto me, Write: for these words are true and faithful. 6.) And he said unto me, It is done. I am Alpha and Omega, the beginning and the end. I will give unto him that is athirst of the fountain of the water of life freely. 7.) He that overcometh shall inherit all things; and I will be his God, and he shall be my son. 8.) But the fearful, and unbelieving, and the abominable, and murderers, and whoremongers, and sorcerers, and idolaters, and all liars, shall have their part in the lake which burneth with fire and brimstone: which is the second death. 9.) And there came unto me one of the seven angels which had the seven vials full of the seven last plagues, and talked with me, saying, Come hither, I will shew thee the bride, the Lamb's wife. 10.) And he carried me away in the spirit to a great and high mountain, and shewed me that great city, the holy Jerusalem, descending out of heaven from God, 11.) Having the glory of God: and her light was like unto a stone most precious, even like a jasper stone, clear as crystal; 12.) And had a wall great and high, and had twelve gates, and at the gates twelve angels, and names written thereon, which are the names of the twelve tribes of the children of Israel: 13.) On the east three gates; on the north three gates; on the south three gates; and on the west three gates. 14.) And the wall of the city had twelve foundations, and in them the names of the twelve apostles of the Lamb. 15.) And he that talked with me had a golden reed to measure the city, and the gates thereof, and the wall thereof. 16.) And the city lieth foursquare, and the length is as large as the breadth: and he measured the city with the reed, twelve thousand furlongs. The length and the breadth and the height of it are equal. 17.) And he measured the wall thereof, an hundred and forty and four cubits, according to the measure of a man, that is, of the angel. 18.) And the building of the wall of it was of jasper: and the city was pure gold, like unto clear glass. 19.) And the foundations of the wall of the city were garnished with all manner of precious stones. The first foundation was jasper; the second, sapphire; the third, a chalcedony; the fourth, an emerald; 20.) The fifth, sardonyx; the sixth, sardius; the seventh, chrysolite; the eighth, beryl; the ninth, a topaz; the tenth, a chrysoprasus; the eleventh, a jacinth; the twelfth, an amethyst. 21.) And the twelve gates were twelve pearls; every several gate was of one pearl: and the street of the city was pure gold, as it were transparent glass. 22.) And I saw no temple therein: for the Lord God Almighty and the Lamb are the temple of it. 23.) And the city had no need of the sun, neither of the moon, to shine in it: for the glory of God did lighten it, and the Lamb is the light thereof. 24.) And the nations of them which are saved shall walk in the light of it: and the kings of the earth do bring their glory and honour into it. 25.) And the gates of it shall not be shut at all by day: for there shall be no night there. 26.) And they shall bring the glory and honour of the nations into it. 27.) And there shall in no wise enter into it anything that defileth, neither whatsoever worketh abomination, or maketh a lie: but they which are written in the Lamb's book of life.

Revelation 21:-1-27

1 And I saw a new heaven and a new earth: for the first heaven and the first earth were passed away; and there was no more sea.

2 And I John saw the holy city, new Jerusalem, coming down from God out of heaven, prepared as a bride adorned for her husband.

3 And I heard a great voice out of heaven saying, Behold, the tabernacle of God is with men, and he will dwell with them, and they shall be his people, and God himself shall be with them, and be their God.

4 And God shall wipe away all tears from their eyes; and there shall be no more death, neither sorrow, nor crying, neither shall there be any more pain: for the former things are passed away.

5 And he that sat upon the throne said, Behold, I make all things new. And he said unto me, Write: for these words are true and faithful.

6 And he said unto me, It is done. I am Alpha and Omega, the beginning and the end. I will give unto him that is athirst of the fountain of the water of life freely.

7 He that overcometh shall inherit all things; and I will be his God, and he shall be my son.

8 But the fearful, and unbelieving, and the abominable, and murderers, and whoremongers, and sorcerers, and idolaters, and all liars, shall have their part in the lake which burneth with fire and brimstone: which is the second death.

9 And there came unto me one of the seven angels which had the seven vials full of the seven last plagues, and talked with me, saying, Come hither, I will shew thee the bride, the Lamb's wife.

10 And he carried me away in the spirit to a great and high mountain, and shewed me that great city, the holy Jerusalem, descending out of heaven from God,

11 Having the glory of God: and her light was like unto a stone most precious, even like a jasper stone, clear as crystal;

12 And had a wall great and high, and had twelve gates, and at the gates twelve angels, and names written thereon, which are the names of the twelve tribes of the children of Israel:

13 On the east three gates; on the north three gates; on the south three gates; and on the west three gates.

14 And the wall of the city had twelve foundations, and in them the names of the twelve apostles of the Lamb.

15 And he that talked with me had a golden reed to measure the city, and the gates thereof, and the wall thereof.

16 And the city lieth foursquare, and the length is as large as the breadth: and he measured the city with the reed, twelve thousand furlongs. The length and the breadth and the height of it are equal.

17 And he measured the wall thereof, an hundred and forty and four cubits, according to the measure of a man, that is, of the angel.

18 And the building of the wall of it was of jasper: and the city was pure gold, like unto clear glass.

19 And the foundations of the wall of the city were garnished with all manner of precious stones. The first foundation was jasper; the second, sapphire; the third, a chalcedony; the fourth, an emerald;

20 The fifth, sardonyx; the sixth, sardius; the seventh, chrysolite; the eighth, beryl; the ninth, a topaz; the tenth, a chrysoprasus; the eleventh, a jacinth; the twelfth, an amethyst.

21 And the twelve gates were twelve pearls; every several gate was of one pearl: and the street of the city was pure gold, as it were transparent glass.

22 And I saw no temple therein: for the Lord God Almighty and the Lamb are the temple of it.

23 And the city had no need of the sun, neither of the moon, to shine in it: for the glory of God did lighten it, and the Lamb is the light thereof.

> 24 *And the nations of them which are saved shall walk in the light of it: and the kings of the earth do bring their glory and honour into it.*
>
> 25 *And the gates of it shall not be shut at all by day: for there shall be no night there.*
>
> 26 *And they shall bring the glory and honour of the nations into it.*
>
> 27 *And there shall in no wise enter into it anything that defileth, neither whatsoever worketh abomination, or maketh a lie: but they which are written in the Lamb's book of life.*

Revelation 21: 11 Having the glory of God: and her light was like unto a stone most precious, even like a jasper stone, clear as crystal;

What an amazing scene being revealed as the wonderful light of the new Jerusalem shines like a precious jasper stone, clear as crystal, but most significantly is the first phrase of verse twelve where it states "having the glory of God. In order to better understand, we can examine the Holy Scriptures to find just how marvelous the glory of God is and how and who the Almighty allowed to see His glorious splendor. In sundry times and in divers manners as expressed in the New Testament book of Hebrews which reveals God's mysterious and master plan throughout time and the various methods and manner He chose to use for bringing forth His ultimate will. One such example involves a heritage so to speak of Gods patterns of the heavenly given to be revealed to His chosen ones in earthly form.

Interestingly, man was made in the image of God, thus the earthly was divinely created by the heavenly. Now if we examine Solomon's temple which was in fact prepared (materials) by David his father who was the chosen of God to lead His people. Amazingly, the Ark of the Covenant which was in the holiest of holies in the temple behind the vail was given by divine instruction for Moses to have built in the exact manner given by God. The ark was set in the holy place with cherubim's facing each other with wings extended overlaid with gold over the ark in its place. The ark was considered so holy that God commanded rings be built into it so staves could be used to lift the ark without being touched by man's hands. Additionally, only the Levitical priests could carry the ark and the ark was to be secured very carefully.

2 Chronicles 5:1-14

> *1.) Thus all the work that Solomon made for the house of the LORD was finished: and Solomon brought in all the things that David his father had dedicated; and the silver, and the gold, and all the instruments, put he among the treasures of the house of God.*

2.) Then Solomon assembled the elders of Israel, and all the heads of the tribes, the chief of the fathers of the children of Israel, unto Jerusalem, to bring up the ark of the covenant of the LORD out of the city of David, which is Zion.

3.) Wherefore all the men of Israel assembled themselves unto the king in the feast which was in the seventh month.

4.) And all the elders of Israel came; and the Levites took up the ark.

5.) And they brought up the ark, and the tabernacle of the congregation, and all the holy vessels that were in the tabernacle, these did the priests and the Levites bring up.

6.) Also king Solomon, and all the congregation of Israel that were assembled unto him before the ark, sacrificed sheep and oxen, which could not be told nor numbered for multitude.

7.) And the priests brought in the ark of the covenant of the LORD unto his place, to the oracle of the house, into the most holy place, even under the wings of the cherubims:

8.) For the cherubims spread forth their wings over the place of the ark, and the cherubims covered the ark and the staves thereof above.

9.) And they drew out the staves of the ark, that the ends of the staves were seen from the ark before the oracle; but they were not seen without. And there it is unto this day.

10.) There was nothing in the ark save the two tables which Moses put therein at Horeb, when the LORD made a covenant with the children of Israel, when they came out of Egypt.

11.) And it came to pass, when the priests were come out of the holy place: (for all the priests that were present were sanctified, and did not then wait by course:

12.) Also the Levites which were the singers, all of them of Asaph, of Heman, of Jeduthun, with their sons and their brethren, being arrayed in white linen, having cymbals and psalteries and harps, stood at the east end of the altar, and with them an hundred and twenty priests sounding with trumpets:)

13.) It came even to pass, as the trumpeters and singers were as one, to make one sound to be heard in praising and thanking the LORD; and when they lifted up their voice with the trumpets and cymbals and instruments of musick, and praised the LORD, saying, For he is good; for his mercy endureth for ever: that then the house was filled with a cloud, even the house of the LORD;

14.) So that the priests could not stand to minister by reason of the cloud: for the glory of the LORD had filled the house of God.

The next event where the glory of God was seen and revealed to holy men who spake as they were moved by the holy ghost was the vision of Isaiah the prophet. The prophet saw the Lord high and lifted up and the angels of God. He also heard the angels cry holy, holy, holy is the Lord of host: the whole earth is full of His glory. The prophet was concerned about being a man of unclean lips and a coal from the altar was brought and touched his lips and it was told him that his sin was purged. Then Isaiah heard the voice of the Lord saying whom shall I send. Isaiah replied here am I send me. The scripture teaches that the Lord revealed to Isaiah about a great forsaking in the midst of the land, but that the holy seed shall return.

Isaiah 6:1-13

1.) *In the year that king Uzziah died I saw also the Lord sitting upon a throne, high and lifted up, and his train filled the temple.*

2.) *Above it stood the seraphims: each one had six wings; with twain he covered his face, and with twain he covered his feet, and with twain he did fly.*

3.) *And one cried unto another, and said, Holy, holy, holy, is the LORD of hosts: the whole earth is full of his glory.*

4.) *And the posts of the door moved at the voice of him that cried, and the house was filled with smoke.*

5.) *Then said I, Woe is me! for I am undone; because I am a man of unclean lips, and I dwell in the midst of a people of unclean lips: for mine eyes have seen the King, the LORD of hosts.*

6.) *Then flew one of the seraphims unto me, having a live coal in his hand, which he had taken with the tongs from off the altar:*

7.) *And he laid it upon my mouth, and said, Lo, this hath touched thy lips; and thine iniquity is taken away, and thy sin purged.*

8.) *Also I heard the voice of the Lord, saying, Whom shall I send, and who will go for us? Then said I, Here am I; send me.*

9.) *And he said, Go, and tell this people, Hear ye indeed, but understand not; and see ye indeed, but perceive not.*

10.) *Make the heart of this people fat, and make their ears heavy, and shut their eyes; lest they see with their eyes, and hear with their ears, and understand with their heart, and convert, and be healed.*

11.) *Then said I, Lord, how long? And he answered, Until the cities be wasted without inhabitant, and the houses without man, and the land be utterly desolate,*

12.) *And the LORD have removed men far away, and there be a great forsaking in the midst of the land.*

13.) *But yet in it shall be a tenth, and it shall return, and shall be eaten: as a teil tree, and as an oak, whose substance is in them, when they cast their leaves: so the holy seed shall be the substance thereof.*

The scripture points to the historical event in the history of His chosen people Israel called the Babylonian captivity. The Lord had warned His people for many years to return to the God of Abraham, Isaac, and Jacob but the leaders and many of the people rejected the mercy of God and turned their backs on their God and refused to hear His messengers, so much so that in one place the bible teaches the Lord told a man of God that the people wouldn't hear Him so they would not hear the messenger either but to tell them anyway. Does a forsaking in the land sound familiar today? Does turning a deaf ear to sound doctrine sound familiar today? God revealed the coming judgment to His servant Isaiah but they still didn't take heed and judgement took place just as it was told by the Word of the Lord. Have people believed a lie today? Has God sent strong delusion already because people did not receive the love of the truth? Does revelation speak of a coming tribulation and final judgement that could be beginning to be experienced even now? How soon could the Lord's return really be? Who does the bible teach will inherit the earth and rule and reign with Christ? What will the world to come, the regeneration, and the thousand year reign of Christ hold?

A warning in the midst of examining some of the instances of the glory of God being manifested before flesh and blood is necessary in order to understand the goodness and the severity of the Almighty Holy One of Israel. On one occasion, the Lord had warned in the Old Testament around the time shortly after the children of Israel had received the law of commandments. The scripture teaches that the Lord had warned to offer incense in the way instructed to the priests who had the charge of the daily sacrifice and not to offer strange fire. However, two sons of Aaron, as the Levites were ordained by God to carry out the office of the priesthood and minister before the Lord the holy sacrifices and offerings, decided to put strange fire from off the altar in the vessels of incense and offer them before God. The Lord struck them both so severely that they died for offering strange fire before the Lord which He commanded not.

Leviticus 10:1-2

1.) *And Nadab and Abihu, the sons of Aaron, took either of them his censer, and put fire therein, and put incense thereon, and offered strange fire before the LORD, which he commanded them not.*

2.) *And there went out fire from the LORD, and devoured them, and they died before the LORD.*

John one verse fourteen: and the Word was made flesh, and dwelt among us, (and we beheld his glory, the glory as of the only begotten of the Father,) full of grace and truth. So, Jesus was the Word made flesh and the disciples and apostles were eye witnesses of His majesty and witnessed first-hand many of the wonderful miracles He did to heal, save, and deliver people from the bondage and snare of the devil. The love of God manifested through His Son Jesus Christ to the world to reconcile the world to Him.

2 Corinthians Chapter 5 verse 19 to wit, that God was in Christ, reconciling the world unto himself, not imputing their trespasses unto them; and hath committed unto us the word of reconciliation.

God truly so truly loved the world that He gave Jesus His only begotten son to be the ultimate sacrifice for the sins of all people whom he had created. Therefore, God highly exalted the Lord Jesus and Jesus is the only name under heaven by which men must be saved. Jesus humbled himself even unto death and the Father exalted Him and hath given Him a name which is above every name. The enemy resisted Daniel before and after God revealed great mysteries to Him during the captivity of the children of Israel. The enemy tried to destroy Jesus after He was born, tempted Jesus in the wilderness, and sought to take His life before He was crucified and rose from the dead and ascended into heaven. Jesus payed a price for you which was His own life. The Lord also seals by His Holy Spirit until the day of redemption of the purchased possession the bible teaches. The Lord's grace and mercy and everlasting love can also reach even unto you.

Revelation 22:17

And the Spirit and the bride say, Come. And let him that heareth say, Come. And let him that is athirst come. And whosoever will, let him take the water of life freely.

Psalms 94:1-23

1.) *O LORD God, to whom vengeance belongeth; O God, to whom vengeance belongeth, shew thyself.*

2.) *Lift up thyself, thou judge of the earth: render a reward to the proud.*

3.) *LORD, how long shall the wicked, how long shall the wicked triumph?*

4.) How long shall they utter and speak hard things? and all the workers of iniquity boast themselves?

5.) They break in pieces thy people, O LORD, and afflict thine heritage.

6.) They slay the widow and the stranger, and murder the fatherless.

7.) Yet they say, The LORD shall not see, neither shall the God of Jacob regard it.

8.) Understand, ye brutish among the people: and ye fools, when will ye be wise?

9.) He that planted the ear, shall he not hear? he that formed the eye, shall he not see?

10.) He that chastiseth the heathen, shall not he correct? he that teacheth man knowledge, shall not he know?

11.) The LORD knoweth the thoughts of man, that they are vanity.

12.) Blessed is the man whom thou chastenest, O LORD, and teachest him out of thy law;

13.) That thou mayest give him rest from the days of adversity, until the pit be digged for the wicked.

14.) For the LORD will not cast off his people, neither will he forsake his inheritance.

15.) But judgment shall return unto righteousness: and all the upright in heart shall follow it.

16.) Who will rise up for me against the evildoers? or who will stand up for me against the workers of iniquity?

17.) Unless the LORD had been my help, my soul had almost dwelt in silence.

18.) When I said, My foot slippeth; thy mercy, O LORD, held me up.

19.) In the multitude of my thoughts within me thy comforts delight my soul.

20.) Shall the throne of iniquity have fellowship with thee, which frameth mischief by a law?

21.) They gather themselves together against the soul of the righteous, and condemn the innocent blood.

22.) But the LORD is my defence; and my God is the rock of my refuge.

23.) And he shall bring upon them their own iniquity, and shall cut them off in their own wickedness; yea, the LORD our God shall cut them off.

REFERENCES

King James Version Online (2021) Revelation ch. 1 verse 8. New Testament. Holy Bible. Retrieved from https://www.kingjamesbibleonline.org/Revelation

Bible.org (2004) The First Five Books. Retrieved from https://bible.org/seriespage

The Dead Sea Scrolls.org (2020) Discovery and Publication. Israel Antiquities Authority. Retrieved from https://www.deadseascrolls.org.

Answers in Genesis (2021) The Flood. Retrieved from https://answersingenesis.org/the-flood/

CBN News (2018) 'Temps as Hot as the Surface of the Sun': Did Scientists Find Evidence of the Destruction of Biblical Sodom. Retrieved from https://www1.cbn.com/cbnnews/cwn/2018/november/

The Federalist Papers (2012) The Mayflower Compact. Retrieved from

https://www.thefederalistpapers.org

ABOUT KHARIS PUBLISHING:

Kharis Publishing, an imprint of Kharis Media LLC, is a leading Christian and inspirational book publisher based in Aurora, Chicago metropolitan area, Illinois. Kharis' dual mission is to give voice to under-represented writers (including women and first-time authors) and equip orphans in developing countries with literacy tools. That is why, for each book sold, the publisher channels some of the proceeds into providing books and computers for orphanages in developing countries, so that these kids may learn to read, dream, and grow. For a limited time, Kharis Publishing is accepting unsolicited queries for nonfiction (Christian, self-help, memoirs, business, health and wellness) from qualified leaders, professionals, pastors, and ministers. Learn more at: About Us - Kharis Publishing - Accepting Manuscript

www.ingramcontent.com/pod-product-compliance
Lightning Source LLC
LaVergne TN
LVHW051525070426
835507LV00023B/3308